HELP
Is **NOT** a
Four-Letter Word

HELP

Is **NOT** a

Four-Letter Word

Why Doing It All Is Doing You In

PEGGY COLLINS

New York   Chicago   San Francisco   Lisbon   London   Madrid   Mexico City
Milan   New Delhi   San Juan   Seoul   Singapore   Sydney   Toronto

1 2 3 4 5 6 7 8 9 10 11 12 13 14 15 16 17 18 19   DOC/DOC   0 9 8 7 6

ISBN-13: 978-0-07-147790-1
ISBN-10:   0-07-147790-X

McGraw-Hill books are available at special quantity discounts to use as premiums and sales promotions, or for use in corporate training programs. For more information, please write to the Director of Special Sales, Professional Publishing, McGraw-Hill, Two Penn Plaza, New York, NY 10121-2298. Or contact your local bookstore.

This book is printed on acid-free paper.

IN MEMORY

of my teacher,
John Mink,
and my mentor,
G. C. (Cleve) Bachman

Contents

Foreword

Self-sufficiency syndrome is a new way to describe a stressful life condition that plagues many hard-working Americans. While self-sufficiency is generally considered something to aspire to, this book describes how, if taken to extremes, it can become a set of behaviors and attitudes that can leave you feeling overwhelmed, exhausted, or unsatisfied. In other words, if not used judiciously, self-sufficiency becomes a negative coping strategy. Much like the concept of perfectionism, which has a good side but is a problem if it becomes a life-guiding principle, self-sufficiency can have costs.

Many self-reliant people recognize the need for interdependence and readily embrace the values of cooperation and collaboration to achieve the goals and meet the needs of others. They eagerly offer their time to work for the greater good. The problem is that when the need is personal, self-sufficients have a double standard, "It is okay for others to accept aid, but I can take care of myself." In this situation, their actions of going it alone do not match with their value of collaboration.

Chapter Seven challenges you to contrast your actions with your values, another intervention strategy commonly used in psychotherapy and in motivational interviewing. A goal of this book is to help you act in a way that is congruent with your basic beliefs. Sometimes that means changing your actions, like acting less self-sufficient and more like a team member. Sometimes it means changing your views, such as deciding that there is more value in interdependence than in going it alone.

What self-sufficients do not realize is that there is no real prize for doing it alone. They get the same rewards (or lack of rewards) as those who operate in a more collaborative fashion and achieve the same goals with far less wear and tear. Seeing this is the key to change. This insightful and revealing book opens the door to inter-dependence. It welcomes in weary self-sufficients and shows them how to find comfort in sharing their burdens with others.

Changing beliefs is difficult to accomplish. You can't just give up the old idea at will. You have to have a good reason for making such a dramatic change. This book helps you to evaluate the pros and cons of believing that you have to be self-sufficient. Through exploration of what drives your self-sufficiency, you might find that the reasons to insist on doing it yourself no longer exist or are outweighed by the disadvantage of continuing to think and act this way.

The strategies for change provided in the latter chapters of the book are those that many cognitive behavior therapists find useful in helping people modify destructive schemas. For example, Ms. Collins encourages readers to become aware of extreme self-sufficiency, and then to rewrite beliefs so that they are more flexible and allow room for asking others to help.

Although reformulated, it is often difficult to make permanent changes in a life-long belief system. The ten steps to making changes described in Chapter Eight will help you to make a transition from the excessively self-sufficient to the sufficient self. They include fo-cusing on the positive nature of your new and more flexible schemas, visualizing how these changes will affect everyday life, and creating an action plan for approaching life without all the restrictions of self-sufficiency. To reinforce your new and healthier attitude, you are en-couraged to observe others who emulate the sufficient self you want to be, seek out encouragers who will support your changes, and celebrate each step along the way.

The self-sufficiency syndrome is a personal and common-sense guide to doing less and enjoying life more. I highly recommend this to perfectionists, workaholics, type-A personalities, and do-it-yourselfers. By reading this book and taking time to consider its message, you will undoubtedly conclude that there is little to lose and much to be gained by being less self-sufficient and enjoying the benefits of interdependence with others.

MONICA RAMIREZ BASCO, PH.D.
DEPARTMENT OF PSYCHOLOGY
UNIVERSITY OF TEXAS AT ARLINGTON

Acknowledgments

Nothing worthwhile is ever done without tremendous support, encouragement, and talent. This book is no exception. I have many people to whom I am eternally grateful. Although words are inadequate, I'd like to extend a heartfelt "Thanks!" to:

Deborah Saverance, whose talent and deep understanding of my subject have made this book the best that it could be.

My agent, Patty Moosbrugger, who believes in getting this word out there as much as I do, and who made it possible for me to do just that.

My family—Sally, Garrett, Jackie, and Janelle—all of whom have taught me what relationships are supposed to be about. And my sister, Norma, who was an encourager and a friend.

My dear friends and speaker support—Lorri Allen, Betty Garrett, and Linda Swindling—whose love, support, and encouragement launched this project and kept it going.

Senior Editor John Aherne, whose patience, generosity, and immense talent guided me every step of the way.

Rena Copperman, Robert S. Tinnon, and Carolyn Wendt—without whom this book would be full of typos and poorly designed.

My friend, writer Jonathan Leach, for the many hours of brainstorming and listening.

Bob and Pat Greenwald, for their friendship and for always having a listening ear and an open heart.

The Hendersonville, North Carolina, JobLink Group, who welcomed me and nurtured me as I went through this process.

All you Self-Sufficients out there, who responded to my surveys, and who spoke up in workshops and let me know I wasn't by myself.

PEGGY COLLINS

——— ————

First and foremost, sincere gratitude to Peggy Collins for the offer and opportunity to coauthor this work with her. Her inspiration and concern for this topic was ignited long before I began collaborating with her in the articulation of it. Her dedication to increasing awareness of the condition she conceived as Self-Sufficiency Syndrome drove this book into reality.

Thanks to Patty Moosbrugger for her marketing efforts, and to Rena Copperman, Carolyn Wendt, Sally Dickson, and Sam Saverance each for their unique contribution to improving and preparing the manuscript. Special thanks to John Aherne, our "shepherding" editor at McGraw-Hill for his guidance, invaluable feedback, and editing expertise. To the friends and family who believed in me and buoyed me up when the tide was low on the voyage, you have my heartfelt appreciation. Among this group, special thanks to Ron and Katie Jones for their unfailing support, the green tea, and the oatmeal cookies. Finally, I want to thank Edgar F. Saverance, who surprised me eight years ago with "Why don't you write a book?" and his son and especially his grandsons, Scott, Sam, and Stephen for the many demonstrations of faith, love, and support—they have way surpassed my expectations... and we all know that's saying a lot!

DEBORAH KENYON SAVERANCE

PART I

Self-Sufficiency Syndrome:
Stuck Out on the Edge,
No Help in Sight

CHAPTER ONE

Stranded on the Seesaw

Choice follows awareness.
JOEL AND MICHELLE LEVEY

"Stand on your own two feet!" You've heard it since you carefully let go of the edge of that coffee table, took those first wobbly steps forward, and fell into Mom or Dad's outstretched arms. And what then? Applause . . . lots of applause!

And oh, the rewards of such risk-taking—a whole new world of moving at will, where you wanted, when you wanted. Sure, you fell a lot, but freedom has its irresistible lure. You whimpered, you got up, you moved on. Why, you even learned how to fall so that those thick layers of diaper absorbed the shock. Very smart kid. Yes, you were on your way to independence and self-sufficiency. Look out, world!

And here you are, all grown up, a mature, functional adult. You've stood on those two feet for decades, and that ability has brought you to where you are today—literally and figuratively. You built a life that includes years of academic education, relationships of your own choosing, and, most likely, a fair amount of professional and financial success.

Yes, you've done well. You are a textbook example of a healthy, normally developing adult human being.

So. . . . What's that? You're waiting for my point? You anticipate there's a "but" that follows all this? (See . . . *still* very smart). Is there a "but" to the benefits of becoming independent? To attaining the hard-earned goal of self-sufficiency?

There is no doubt that the abilities to find your own way in life, to rely on yourself, to set and reach your personal goals are healthy qualities and define a productive, contributing citizen of society. And that's what we're looking for. Friends, neighbors, coworkers, leaders who understand and take personal responsibility for their lives, right? Right. No buts about it.

But, take a second and ask yourself these questions: Have you often felt that you really needed a little help but just couldn't bring yourself to ask for it? Have you ever watched yourself or people you know act as if they have to do *everything* themselves, and all by themselves? Have you ever been offered help that you sorely needed but heard yourself say, "No thanks, I can do it myself"?

What about stress? Do you feel that, for some reason, you're coping with more than your fair share, yet, if you're honest, you know you sort of ask for it? You can hardly resist stepping up to the plate to take on another responsibility—to help out whomever or whatever needs you—in a way that makes you a shining example of a job well done, each and every time.

Have you ever felt that all this stress might be fueling your journey on a runaway train to burnout? No . . . you don't think so . . . it's not *that* bad. Okay . . . maybe it's not . . . and maybe it is. Try some more questions.

Have you ever planned and supervised an event, coordinating all the details for a terrific outcome, and when everyone was present and having a great time, you (the person who made it happen) felt like you were on the outside looking in? Politely acknowledged but kind of isolated? Providing the party but not really a part of it? What we call "feeling alone in a crowd"?

Or how about this? Did you ever need some new skill or information, but instead of admitting it and asking someone you knew to train or educate you, you went underground? You found a book or Internet source, or paid a teacher to tutor you privately on the side, so no one would discover what you didn't know. You could retreat into some kind of crash-course cocoon and emerge looking like you knew it all the time.

All of these situations and many more I could mention illustrate a point. It is possible to be too independent for your own good. It *is* possible to be so totally self-reliant that you cut yourself off from support. And it *is* possible to be so severely self-sufficient that you get stuck somewhere you don't really want to be.

If any of this sounds uncomfortable and familiar, you may feel like protesting and singing, "How can something so right go so wrong?" After all, you've done what was expected—they told you to stand on your own two feet and you have. Who knew you'd rub up so many blisters in the process?

If I sound familiar with this plight, it's because I am. My two feet were covered with Band-Aids for years as the result of some of the stress described above. Of course, no one knew—after all, I would not be self-sufficient if I let on that I was hurting. No, I would keep on doing everything myself, all by myself. That's the vicious cycle we can, with all good intentions, work ourselves into. But it's not necessary. That's what this book is all about. To make you aware of the downside of being severely self-sufficient before you get stuck. To offer assistance in getting free if you are stuck. To suggest that it's okay, actually *more* than okay, to ask for help from the right people at the right time, and to teach you how to do it elegantly and with dignity. To propose that reaching independence is not the final destination in personal human development. That as good as it is to stand on your own two feet, you can carry forward the strengths of your rugged independence and reach a more balanced place that isn't an isolated uphill trek. Interested? Hit a chord? Then read on for the secrets of tweaking your life to this better place.

Where We're Going

This book was written for you or for someone you know and care about who cannot break free from the need to do it all, all by themselves—for those well-intentioned, hardworking souls who have ended up stuck in the cycle of extreme self-sufficiency. In these pages you'll be offered new information and perspective on what is often treated as a sacred cow in Western culture: the attribute of self-sufficiency. I'll explain:

- The signs and symptoms of Self-Sufficiency Syndrome. Learn how such a fundamental strength can turn on us.
- How it's possible to get stuck in a life of severe self-sufficiency. Explore how and why you can become so separate, so isolated that you no longer find it within yourself to ask for help, even when you sorely need it.
- How to evaluate your level of self-sufficiency. Assess whether it's serving you well in living a life that matches your values and goals.
- How to balance accomplishments with relationships. You will see how your behavior has been accomplishment-driven because of your inability to depend on others.
- How to stop the cycle and get unstuck. Discover how to move away from an extreme position of self-sufficiency toward a more moderate, balanced state in which you retain your healthy self-reliance but provide yourself with alternatives for support when you want and need it.
- How, when, and from whom to ask for help. Learn the language of asking for help in a way that allows you to stay in charge of your life while building strong collaborative and communal relationships.

- How to know when to stand and when to lean: the strength
  of interdependence. See how living more interdependently
  offers you the opportunity to enjoy more liberty, greater freedom, and deeper, more meaningful relationships.

Where We're Not Going

There are probably a few things I should clarify up front. As we
look at the topic of self-sufficiency, I am *definitely* not going to
imply that the character qualities that make our free society
great—self-reliance, stoicism, courage in the face of adversity, the
pursuit of excellence—are in question as to their fundamental
value in our history, for today, and for our future.

No, consider this a road map sketched out to guide you to a
place of further growth that can be reached only *after* having
attained a healthy measure of raw, rugged, stick-to-it self-reliance.
This is your invitation to journey with me as we look on up the
path to the summit of interdependence, a place where we are both
strongly separate and vitally connected. It's the best of both worlds
and worth every step. Are you coming?

Stranded on the Seesaw

To get someplace new, it's good to get a lock on where we are now,
and maybe an idea about how we got here. When I was a kid, I
loved seesaws. We happened to be in Santa Maria, California, the
year I started school. If I concentrate, I can still smell the orange
blossoms on the tree that grew by my bedroom window.

The first grade was an exciting year for me. I loved school and, of course, recess. We'd race to get dibs on the playground equipment. Others could have the slides and swings; the seesaw was first choice for me and my best friend. Now, seesaws were quite different then; they weren't the sleek metal ones you see today. The one I went for was made of a large, thick wooden plank. There were no handles. You just grasped the sides for dear life and tried not to get a splinter.

One particular day, I remember clearly, my friend and I had made a beeline to the seesaw, and as we were taking turns soaring like birds up into the sky, something across the playground pulled her attention away. As her end of the seesaw came to the ground, suddenly, without explanation or warning, she jumped off, and you know the results. I fell with a sharp, hard thud, startled, frightened, blinking back tears and looking around to see if anyone had witnessed my humiliation.

Strange, isn't it, how a picture from your past will stick with you? I didn't know it that day, but that seesaw experience became a metaphor for how I was to live almost forty years of my life. A combination of many distressful childhood experiences convinced me that other people, no matter how well intentioned, couldn't be trusted to take good care of me and keep me safe. So, at about nine or ten years old, I decided I would forever and always do it myself. That way, I wouldn't be subject to the whims, inconsideration, or neglect of others. I would put all my expectations on me, someone over whom I had complete control. And you know what? In many ways, this worked. I grew up and flourished, making my place academically and excelling in all kinds of competitive activities (you really didn't want to be on my opposing side in a high school debate!).

This pattern of accomplishment carried on into adulthood. Working my way into professional management and leadership positions where lucrative compensation was a given. Branching out into corporate consulting, speaking, and training employees in numerous Fortune 500 companies. Rearing two beautiful, healthy children into adulthood as a single mom fully invested in supporting the PTA and all their many extracurricular activities. Yes, I would take good care of myself and anyone or anything I was responsible for—that was my role, that was my purpose, that was my source of personal self-worth. I was what I achieved, so I drove myself to achieve a lot—all by myself.

When I looked in the mirror, I saw the reflection of a woman who was self-sufficient.

In Defense of Self-Sufficiency

What's so bad about being self-sufficient? Not a thing! That is, if by self-sufficient you mean becoming *self-reliant*, which we'll define as demonstrating the will and ability to take responsibility for yourself.

Not only is learning self-sufficiency not bad, it's a natural and essential component of developing into a mature adult and a productive citizen in society. We all know that growing up means learning to pull our own weight. We applaud those who do and get impatient with those who don't—especially when they can but won't. We all know what a compliment it is to be praised for our "work ethic"—and, honestly, is there any stronger insult in our contemporary culture than to be labeled with the most dreaded of four-letter words, *lazy*?

I guess you could say that learning self-sufficiency is a required course in the developmental curriculum of our first few decades. And, goodness knows, it can take a lot of effort, guidance, and support, along with an occasional skinned knee and broken heart, to earn a passing grade. Granted, it's easier for some than others, but we all learn through a process of observation and some degree of trial and error what it means to accept responsibility for ourselves. And we are all working with the same basic three components.

The Big Three

Three things combined determine how we turn out as adults:

1. Genetics
2. Environment
3. Personal choice

There's not a lot we can do about the first two. Even with all the advances in genetics, we still can't pick our own, so we have no choice but to be elated with or resigned to the genetic code we were given. It follows, of course, that we can't pick our own parents, culture, ethnicity, nationality, or economic status at birth. We are pushed out into the world to land in the arms of whoever is there to catch us. And, although as infants we have a tremendous capacity to learn and develop physically, cognitively, and emotionally, we are dependent on parents, family, and society to provide the essentials (food, shelter, safety, nurturing, and so on). We have no say in what these combined circumstances will be—they are the proverbial "hand that we're dealt."

Ah, but then there's number three, the magic ingredient of the human condition: personal choice. We get to choose how we play the hand we're dealt. *Play*—an action verb—denotes having freedom to consider and choose an option among alternatives. Even in some of the most oppressive and limiting of environments, human beings have a degree of choice in how they will act, react, and cope with or overcome obstacles. And we start practicing this in our high chairs when we push our milk cup splattering to the floor so we can venture a grasp at sister's interesting bowl of cereal.

There is so much potential in the power of choice. Aren't we constantly intrigued by stories of individuals who were handed every advantage by birth (a royal flush, so to speak), and then they ... well, just fold? Don't we want to join in a collective cheer when we learn of what some people manage to make of their lives when originally dealt a mere pair of twos? Granted, most of us are somewhere in the middle, where figuring out how to make wise choices is an ongoing, lifelong challenge. But free will itself is a birthright to be cherished and to be used to temper or enhance the luck of the draw of heredity and environment.

What about those periods of your life when you can't choose, because you don't know and can't understand how to look after yourself? When you think about it, it's really quite a miracle that any of us reaches a degree of self-sufficiency. What utterly helpless little creatures our species produces at birth. We start out totally dependent—but that, too, is not only normal, it's essential.

Stage One: Dependency—
The Critical Foundation

Understanding the Life Span of
Human Development—Ph.D. Not Required

As you've probably figured out by now, this is not a book for academics. It's for real people who use their intelligence, street smarts, and good old common sense to figure out what's up. That being said, we've come to have pretty reliable ideas about how we grow up, based on the hard-earned research of sincere social and behavioral scientists over the past hundred years. The names of some of these folks may ring a distant bell in your mental archive from Psych or Sociology 101: Freud, Erikson, Piaget, Bandura, Bowlby, Ainsworth, and so forth.

Each of these lauded social scientists had his or her own unique slant on how we develop from infants to adults. But, if we were able to enlist the use of a time machine and could gather them all around a discussion table, they would all agree to a large degree with this: *What happens to us when we are totally dependent children forms the influential foundation for how we interact with our world for the rest of our lives.* Here's the layperson version of what most of the developmental research concludes:

- How we think, act, and feel as independent adults is built upon the foundation of our experience as dependent children.
- During our dependent years, our primary caregivers influence our view of the world and ourselves in the world.
- In the optimal situation, young children are able to develop a sense of secure belonging that enables them to try out independent behavior without risk of losing their safety net of attachment and approval with primary caregivers.
- One of the significant questions of a developing child is, "Who and what can I trust?" The answer to that question determines whether one sees the world as a safe or scary place.
- As adults, we will seek to compensate or provide for ourselves, consciously or unconsciously, the essential needs that were not met for us as dependent children.

What's Taking So Long?

Of all mammals, we humans have the longest period of development before assuming adulthood. Why is that? We are born with the biggest brains, primed to sponge and assimilate enormous amounts of information during our early years. But compared to our fellow primates we are the slowest in being able to fend for ourselves. It takes years before we can supply our basic needs of food, safety, and shelter.

In their book, *The Irreducible Needs of Children*, childhood experts and doctors T. Berry Brazelton and Stanley I. Greenspan explain that this long period of dependency is so that human beings can develop their psychological capacities under the protection and care of others. They go on to present seven basic requirements that ensure healthy development of emotional, social, and intellectual abilities in kids. The first on this list is "the need for ongoing nurturing relationships." Just as vital as the obvious needs for food, shelter, physical safety, and protection from illness and injury is the need for the kind of nurturing that will allow the brain to develop the capacities for intellectual and social growth.

That means how we are cared for impacts the chemistry and neuron growth of the brain. That means we're totally dependent during the most critical time in our lives—those first few years when our oversize human brains are developing at the greatest rate to prepare for a lifetime of servicing all of our thoughts, actions, sensations, and emotions as adults. Think about it: all this occurs before we have the capacity to even remember it. Not an ounce of personal choice is involved—now, that's totally dependent, and totally normal.

In a Perfect World

It goes without saying that all this really puts the pressure on good old Mom and Dad. The most important task that a child and caregivers accomplish during the dependent stage of life is getting attached. From the moment we are born, we are looking for Mom. As babies, we are constantly taking in images, building a basis to interpret them, and experiencing very intense feelings.

In a perfect world, we learn to feel safe when our caregiver is available and responsive to us, and we learn how to get helpful responses when we need something. That's what all the crying is about—it's our best shot at communicating before we have words. In a perfect world, getting love reliably and consistently makes us feel worthy of love, and the perception that we can attain what we need from those around us allows us to sense even as a small child that we can have an impact on our world. We develop a foundation of trust that assures us that our caregivers are there for us, and thus the world is a safe place to move in and explore. If things go awry in our explorations, we can run back to base (Mom) and regain our sense of security. This is called being securely attached, and in a perfect world we all would be because we know now that the type of attachment we develop as small children carries over to how we see and behave in the world as adults. You know, whether we see ourselves as okay, autonomous, lovable, competent, and others as dependable and trustworthy.

How does this matter in addressing your current situation? Only to the extent that it could shed light on the pattern of development that may influence how you look at things now. Congratulations if your childhood was perfect; for one reason or another most of us have to manage with less than ideal, and we do a darn good job. And the good news for most of us is that the impact of early attachment on our adult behavior is not out of our control. Whether or not we come out of our youth with what the social scientists call a *secure base* as an adult is not, I repeat, not a yes/no proposition. Studies show that the key quality of secure, autonomous adults is not that they had secure attachments with their parents but that they were open and coherent in reflecting and working through the less than ideal aspects of their dependent stage. There's that component of personal choice again!

Stage Two: Independence— The Essential Transition

It's the fall of your freshman year in college, and independence has taken on a whole new meaning. You're liberated. You can go where you want, eat what you want, and stay up all night anytime you want. Why, out from under the scrutiny of Mom and Dad, you can even run with scissors! You are your own man, your own woman.

———   ———

Of course, technically, maybe you can't claim to be totally self-sufficient since it was either Uncle Sam or your parents who signed off on your college tuition bill. And that part-time job you had for "living" expenses (like pizza, beer, dates, and rock concerts) during college was a position reserved for students.

Chances are that even if you're balking at the situation above, having worked *your* way through school with *no help* from anybody, you probably know someone who fits this scenario. It's pretty common nowadays. The point is this: in hindsight, we can all chuckle and confess that becoming independent involved a whole set of transitional experiences in which we were gradually responsible for our decisions and their consequences. Independence required a healthy amount of self-sufficiency.

Becoming independent is essential in the growth process. It is where we're headed from the time we're toddlers. From one end of the seesaw to the other. Our culture and educational institutions seek to instill and encourage independence from kindergarten on with the goal of preparing us to get a job, pay taxes, and generally take care of ourselves without much assistance. For most of us who became severely self-sufficient, our transition to independence came early on.

There were roles and responsibilities we were expected to assume, and we did. We were often viewed as little adults. Serious, focused, directed, planning for tomorrow, looking after everybody, making our own decisions without much consultation, taking the initiative to do the next thing—these were the characteristics that became second nature.

We took care of ourselves, we were dependable, we were strong. We learned lessons that prepared us well for the inevitable ups and downs of adult life. And somewhere along the way many of us came to the conclusion that this is what we were here for, this was our purpose, that being independent and as self-sufficient as possible was as good as it got.

Now I want to tread carefully when it comes to the topic of independence—gosh knows, I cherish mine. Always have. Ask anyone who knows me. Like I explained, I've been pretty much running my own show since I was nine. The concept of becoming independent is part of the very fiber of our culture. I make a concerted effort to never take for granted the blessing of living in a free society in a time when the barriers of gender, race, ethnicity, and socioeconomic status are diminished. And I'm proud to be a part of a culture that continues to work on reaching a higher standard in these areas—a higher standard of liberty for all.

What I had to learn was where the values of independence and self-sufficiency fit in my personal growth and development. I had always thought of independence as the ultimate goal of the game, the trophy going to the most independent, most self-sufficient, which of course I strived to be. Came pretty darn close, too, until I hit a wall. After many puzzling years, I got a piece of information that changed my perspective. The adjustment I had to make in my thinking was that becoming independent was an essential and important *stage* in my personal development rather than the end *destination*. It wasn't the end but part of the process, the second event of a triathlon that prepares you for the third. This little insight took me, oh, about forty years to learn. They didn't teach it in school, certainly not in my professional world where everyone looks out for herself and you better watch your back. This book is my attempt to let you in on it a little earlier.

But back to those forty years. What happened you ask? I got stuck. Really stuck. So stuck in doing it all, all by myself, so afraid to ask for help, so afraid to even *look* like I needed to ask for help, that I . . . well, I get ahead of myself. All I want at this point is for you to consider any similarities in your own life or someone you know who seems to be so self-sufficient he or she just cannot ask for help. What I want you to understand is that there is hope— there is more—you are not at your final destination. I intend to provide a roadmap. There may be some rough pavement on the way, but you won't be alone. And since I've gone the long way, you can be sure I'll provide you with every shortcut I can.

What's the starting point of our journey? The place where you may be stuck: way out on the far end of that seesaw. We're going to stop now, take a deep breath and reflect back at how we managed to get in this sticky position. Everyone has his or her own story, but underneath the details there typically lies a similar thesis: I am responsible for everything and everybody in my world and failing in fulfillment of these responsibilities is not an option. For example, let me tell you about two kids that you may have known growing up, Jack and Barbara.

CHAPTER TWO

Signs and Symptoms of Severe Self-Sufficiency

It is true that no one can harm the person
who wears armor. But no one can help him either.
KRISTIN HUNTER

Jack's Story

The whole class looks at Jack when his name is called to come to the principal's office. Jack is an honor student, class officer, and basketball star, so no one can imagine that he is in trouble. He isn't—his brother, Brian, two years younger, is—again. Second time this week. That's after Brian was sent home last month when he was caught cheating on an exam. This time he's being given detention for being disruptive and unruly in class—and Brian is not taking his sentence calmly. The principal had tried but once again couldn't reach Jack's parents at work. Jack knows Dad is on a project in New York and Mom is in court all afternoon. He needs to step in and be surrogate parent again. As he listens to the principal's complaint, he feels hot and embarrassed by Brian's disrespectful behavior. He wants to protect his kid brother and punch him out at the same time. But, like he did on Tuesday, he sits down and tells Brian to pull it together and stop acting like a jerk. And as always, Brian complies—Jack is his hero. Brian agrees to apologize to his science teacher and show up for detention after school. As Jack walks to his class, twenty minutes late, he decides there's no need to bug his parents about the incident. They're overwhelmed at work and already worried about Brian. He'd handled this and will do it again if necessary. No one has told him, but he knows it's his job.

Barbara's Story

Barbara always avoids her friends who gather at the flagpole after school to gab, gossip, and giggle. She knows they'll ask her to join in, and she can't—she must go straight home. It's only three blocks. If she doesn't dawdle, she can make it in ten minutes, well before her brothers get home. Mom needs her help—she's been sick for quite a while, and sometimes she drinks during the day to make herself feel better. Barbara prays it's been a good day, and Mom will be dressed and have something thawed for dinner. Then Barb can get the laundry done that was left all over her brothers' floor before she starts her homework. Of course, if it was a bad day, she'll need to think about what leftovers can be warmed up for supper. She needs to hurry to see what she'll need to make just before Dad gets home. He'll be tired and hungry.

What's Normal, Anyway?

Maybe you didn't have the good fortune of being looked after in a way that paid much attention to your need for a healthy dependent stage. Maybe you knew you had to become self-sufficient before you even learned how to pronounce the word. Or maybe, although you appeared to experience a normal transition from independence to self-reliance, you can't remember a time when you weren't convinced that you were responsible for everything, that it was up to you to look after yourself and everyone else in your charge and to do it error-free. All mistakes were big mistakes—your mistakes, not to be repeated and, if possible, not to be revealed. The upside is that you learned to be strong and trustworthy, attributes to be admired. The downside is that you learned to judge your total worth on any given day by what you did right or well the day before. You were what you did, you were adequate or inferior depending on your most recent performance, and, therefore, you were driven to perform well. You had to. Others could get by with being average or good—you had to be excellent to even be included with the others. More was required of you, and you learned to meet this challenge. Your biggest fear was that something or somebody might step in and disturb the delicate balance of your life.

Have you ever said to yourself, I must:

- stay in control and protect myself from disappointment or misfortune
- prove to myself that I am all I need
- be able to make it without anyone else . . . because, in fact, I might have to
- be self-sufficient
- be severely self-sufficient because it's like money in the bank

Don't misunderstand. There's nothing wrong with a little security. Or gritting your teeth and doing what you have to do to get through bad times. No, there's absolutely nothing wrong with that.

So, what's the problem?

Amy's Story

The sauce for Amy's dinner party bubbles on the stove. The house is immaculate, the table is set, and everything is just about ready. Amy decides it's a good time to arrange the flowers that will serve as the centerpiece. She wants to use her mother's crystal vase, the one she keeps up in the top cabinet in her kitchen. Now, reaching anything in that cabinet would be a challenge, even if Amy weren't petite. She takes a chair from the kitchen table and stands on it. No luck: the vase is still well out of reach. *No problem*, she thinks. She climbs down from the chair, retrieves a plastic step stool from her daughter's bathroom, then balances the stool on the seat of the chair. Now, if she stretches on tiptoe, Amy can *just* reach the vase and . . . oops, a new problem. She feels a sickening "give" under her feet, and glances down in time to see the surface of the stool (meant for a toddler, not an adult) beginning to crack. By jerking both feet outward, to the edges of the stool, and wobbling on her tiptoes, she is just able to grasp the vase.

"What *are* you doing?" Amy's husband enters the kitchen and dashes toward her.

"I'm okay—everything's under control," she grunts, straining to secure the vase. Suddenly, the stool shatters. Amy leaps clear of her makeshift ladder to the floor, clutching the vase over her head like a trophy.

Her husband studies her, the overturned chair, the shattered step stool, the vase.

"You know," he says, shaking his head, "you could have saved yourself a whole lot of grief. I was right in the living room. Why didn't you call me to get that for you?"

"What for?" she says, noticing a sharp, unfamiliar twinge in her right ankle. Limping toward the cut flowers that lie waiting in the sink, she dismisses the whole incident, "No need to bother you—I got it down just fine."

True story and just one example of the illustrations people have provided from their real lives about an automatic pattern of predictable behavior I'm calling *Self-Sufficiency Syndrome*. Evaluate Amy's behavior. Would you call it reasonable, resourceful, admirable, crazy, or all of the above?

The Big Picture: From a Strength to a Weakness

In the real world, some of us go without the external help we need to build our best self. Thankfully, the human psyche has the capacity to step up to its own plate and, to a certain degree, provide for itself the belief, guidance, education, discipline, security, and acknowledgment that would ideally come from our caretakers in our early years.

If the truth really could be told, it wouldn't surprise me if the majority of us had our ideal bubble burst early on. Why? Because our parents were human, as were theirs, and humans make mistakes. In fact, it feels a bit disingenuous to shake a finger at our parents when most of us would feel a little breeze behind us stirred up by our kids shaking their fingers at us. We all fail when it comes to providing an ideal, fully supportive, and thoroughly nurturing twenty-year maturation incubator for our offspring. However, degrees do matter—some parents falter much more seriously than others. There is a big difference between well-intentioned mistakes of ignorance or misinformation and actions that purposefully harm, neglect, or degrade children. We call the former, stupidity; we call the latter, abuse. In this context, I'm happy and relieved to say, "Just call me Stupid."

There is a bit of comfort knowing that most of us are in the same dealing-with-our-childhood boat together. There comes a point when the results we carry from our parents' less-than-perfect parenting become our problems to figure out—and if we choose, to learn to resolve in our own lives and even break the cycle of passing the unpleasantness on to the next generation.

A complication in this process is that sometimes the solutions we adopt to weather our early years have a short half-life. Hopefully, they rescue us from the really bad stuff and move us down the road of life to a safer place.

However, over time, these same coping behaviors may start producing diminishing returns—until one day we realize we are stuck in a place we never intended to be. That's the kind of solution self-sufficiency can be when it becomes severe. It becomes a core perspective that drives a person to prove to the world that he can make it alone. He's only truly worthy if he sees himself doing it all, all by himself. Asking for help is not an option or is, at the most, the very last resort when there is no other alternative. When I say no other, I mean no other. The stories I could tell about how far some people will go before asking for assistance are hard to believe.

I do find comfort in knowing that I have pretty good company in grabbing on to severe self-sufficiency to help row myself through the whitewater of my youth. One of the esteemed psychological minds of recent decades, M. Scott Peck, author of the bestselling *The Road Less Traveled* and more than fifteen other works, described using the same survival solution, only he called it "excessive independence." He told his own story of how the roots of this trait came from a childhood with parents who were "generally decent but often over-controlling."

To have been significantly dependent on [my parents] would have been to place myself in a position where I would be steamrolled out of my own identity. For my psychological survival I had to keep my psychic distance from them. I could do this only through the development of an unconscious motto of independence: "Who needs them? Who needs anyone?"

I bet a lot of us can identify with this approach to similar developmental stress. We do what we have to do, think what we have to think, deny what we have to deny to get through the years when we're vulnerable. We usually make it through intact, but not without side effects from our self-sufficiency solution. Dr. Peck seemed to concur:

Neuroses, however, are not like little pebbles you simply kick out of your path once you recognize them. Rather they are like huge boulders one has to keep chipping away at for a lifetime. So it is today, twenty-five years later, I am still too slow in asking for help when I need it and in accepting it when it is offered—much, much better at it, but still handicapped. On a Sunday morning, not too many years ago when I was still in practice, I was coming out of church with a patient, Susan, after it had started pouring rain. Susan's car was parked close to the church; mine was a hundred yards up the road. When we reached hers, Susan said, "Here, Scotty, take my umbrella. You can give it back to me at our appointment on Wednesday."

"That's all right," I replied, refusing her. "I don't need it." And I didn't really. I was but slightly drenched by the time I reached my own car. It was only when I had driven several miles toward home that I realized the significance of the event. "You've done it again, haven't you, Scotty?" I said to myself. "Dammit, you've done it again." I had sinned once more. It was not merely that I did need her umbrella; more important, I had unnecessarily rejected Susan. It would have made her feel good to have made the loan, but I had blown the opportunity, that little momentary call. It was an act of incivility on my part. I had blockaded the web of exchange.

I think we'd all cut Dr. Peck some slack—not taking the umbrella was not a criminal offense—but he did illustrate how pervasive the severely self-sufficient mind-set can become in all the little nooks and crannies of our everyday responses. When a pattern of behavior that doesn't serve us well is so entrenched that we practice it automatically, then we've got a problem. Who knew we could get stuck in a state of "excessive independence"—a state where we automatically and sometimes involuntarily practice the extreme pattern of Self-Sufficiency Syndrome.

When I think of someone suffering from severe self-sufficiency, I get a funny picture in my head. I picture this well-dressed businessperson in an Armani suit wearing one of those large, white, round life preservers around the waist. Not exactly tasteful accessorizing, so the look does catch your attention. The story behind the picture is that evidently this individual was in a shipwreck as a kid and was lucky enough to grab hold of this thing while spitting, coughing, and choking for air, and the device floated the child to safety. That's the good news. The bad news is that the trauma of this ordeal caused the kid to be, shall we say, very attached to the life preserver. Like Linus with his blanket or me with my American Express card, he would not dream of leaving home without it for fear of drowning the next time.

Well, the kid grew, but the life preserver didn't, and I'll be darned if the thing didn't get stuck around his waist—now he has to get dressed around it, stuffing his shirt down, tugging his waistband up under the tight white hoop. Not very comfortable, granted, but, he reasons, one has to make concessions to be secure.

He is actually a friendly, personable guy, but, as you can imagine, he can't really engage in intimate conversation—not with that big old yellowing life preserver bumping into everything and everybody. Oh, yes indeed, he maintains his personal space with no trouble at all—others are forced to keep their distance. I guess you could say he "stands alone in a crowd" in exercising his solution for feeling safe, secure, and in control. It's just that his reaction is way out of proportion to the threat, wouldn't you agree?

I know you get the picture and the point. What serves us well at one stage of life may need to be released or revised at another stage of life. It is possible to carry something helpful so far out of original context that it becomes ill fitting in your developmental process. *A strength from the past can be misapplied in the present to the point of becoming a weakness.* Self-Sufficiency Syndrome fits that category.

Hello, My Name Is Peggy, and I'm a Self-Sufficient

My dad was a troubleshooter for General Motors, and General Motors must have had a lot of trouble, because we moved every year—sometimes twice—coast to coast and back again. I went to seventeen different schools in twelve years.

My dad would be on the road all week, come home on Friday, crawl into a bottle, and not come out until Monday, when it was time to go on the road again.

Now, when you grow up in an alcoholic home with parents who didn't always get along, and you're moving all the time, you lose touch with what's normal. You might say that I grew up in a self-sufficiency incubator. I remember deciding when I was nine or ten that if this was what normal was, well then, "so help me—I'd better learn to take care of myself." And I did. That was the fork in my developmental road.

By 1987, I was a self-supporting single mom with two small children. Although I worked full-time in a career involving extensive travel, I prided myself on "being there" for my kids and actively participating in their schools. Simultaneously, it fell to me to attend to the growing needs of my elderly parents during a time when the unexpected end of a nine-year relationship with the man in my life had me reeling inside. I guess you could say I had a lot going on. But I was determined to keep things under control. I insisted on being strong.

A little before noon one day in February, I found myself standing in my office's restroom, pressing my face and hands against the marble walls. I had escaped my office but didn't know how I had gotten here. I had been sitting at my desk when suddenly my hands began to tremble. It felt as if my heart were slamming against my ribs. I was lightheaded. *Heart attack*, I thought—but there was no pain, just the racing of my heart, and an eerie sensation that the walls were closing in on me. I was overwhelmed by an unexplainable fear. I thought I was going to die. I had never experienced anything like this in my life, and I felt utterly powerless.

The cold marble steadied me. I forced myself to take deep breaths. After what seemed like an eternity, I was able to walk to the basin and splash cold water on my face. Friends had arranged to meet me for lunch, and it was time to be going.

Riding down in the elevator, I debated: Lunch, or hospital? Hospital, or lunch? My heart continued to race. When the doors opened, I had decided to keep my lunch date. At the restaurant, I began to feel a little calmer, but things were still not right. One by one, as my friends approached the table and said hello, I saw worry and alarm in their eyes.

"Are you all right?" asked Rachel. "You look so *pale*."

"Of course," I answered unconvincingly. "I'm just a little winded."

But—friends that they were, and are to this day—they knew better. With care and compassion, they pressed me for answers.

Sensations are heightened when you are in crisis. Today, I remember that noonday conversation as though it were happening at this moment—every sound, every color, every word. I remember how difficult it was for me, who had never even admitted to having a hangnail, to acknowledge that something was dreadfully wrong. I also remember how good it felt to start talking. Every detail of that morning came pouring out. When I finished, it felt as if I had just dumped a thousand jigsaw-puzzle pieces on the table. There was relief, but also exhaustion and confusion. I was desperate to know what it all meant.

After a pause, my friend Holly said quietly, "It sounds like you had a panic attack." Holly went on to say that another friend of hers had such attacks regularly. She said her friend's experiences matched my own, and that it was important for me to get to a doctor right away.

The doctor's visit proved Holly right. Yes, what I had suffered was a classic panic attack. With time and treatment, things would improve. But my real awakening had already happened. My epiphany occurred the day before, in the immediate aftermath of the attack. As much as I wanted to travel back in time, to go back to a moment when I had felt totally in charge, I knew in the deepest part of myself that that was not to be. I knew that my panic attack had been the outcome of a lifetime of needing desperately to have everything under control—that it was my very need to be in control that had triggered my attack. And life just kept piling on more for me to try to stay in control of. My body couldn't take it anymore.

In my zeal to maximize my strengths—my independence, my capacity to assume responsibility, my ability to get things done—I had let those unchecked strengths bring me to a place of weakness. Now, as I peeked out from beneath the rubble of my life, I knew that something had to change—and that something was myself. Without knowing the words for it, without understanding that such a thing existed, I recognized that I was a Self-Sufficient.

You're Not Alone

In boardrooms and ballrooms, in small cities and large, whenever I identify myself as a Self-Sufficient, a kind of electric spark goes through the room. I hear people say instantly, "That's me!" Or they come up to me afterward and say something like, "Until you talked about it just now, I didn't realize that's what I was." They then tell me their own stories. When I suggest that their level of self-sufficiency may have become not a hallmark of emotional health, but an overwhelming burden in their life, I see the light of recognition in their eyes. Like me, they have never thought of self-sufficiency as anything but an appropriate way of being in a world in which more is better. It doesn't occur to them that they can be too self-sufficient for their own good.

What has become clear to me as I've introduced this topic over and over is that Self-Sufficients are everywhere. We are homemakers and office workers, lawyers and artists, scientists and social workers, college students and athletes, executives and CEOs, moms and dads. Wherever you look, you are likely to see someone who appears to have the world on a string—but is strung out under the facade. While the Self-Sufficient appears to have supreme control over her life, in truth she is always anxious about her performance and often retreats behind her private unseen wall, away from judging eyes, to build the sort of image she desires to project in public. She avoids any situation where she may have to stand in the spotlight and risk being laughed at, criticized, shamed, or ridiculed. She tells herself, "I will not allow myself to be judged for what I don't know, can't do, or can't master—therefore, I will protect myself by going behind closed doors and learning whatever I must to make myself enough, all by myself." You can't fault her for wanting some privacy, but the walls Self-Sufficients construct not only shield and protect, they isolate, disconnect, and alienate them from others—even well-meaning others who are ready to help if asked. This defensive fortress-building taken to an extreme can become a form of self-sabotage that cuts her off from the love, support, companionship, and collaboration she could enjoy. The wall blockades "the web of exchange" that Dr. Peck talked about. What was meant to be a safe house to keep others out becomes a kind of comfortable cell where she locks away all her vulnerabilities for no one to see.

I remember the topic coming up with a successful male colleague of mine at a conference we were both attending. After batting the concept of severe self-sufficiency back and forth, I asked him point-blank if he thought this was perhaps just a woman's issue. His emphatic reply was, "Are you kidding? I attended an outbound retreat recently and couldn't allow myself to fall back into the arms of my team." That required just too much trust— too much vulnerability.

And then, guys, there's also that little problem of asking for directions.

Q & A

Q: If Self-Sufficiency Syndrome is such a serious problem, why haven't we heard about it before?

A: Perhaps because severe self-sufficiency has so few negative consequences for anyone other than the Self-Sufficient himself (and the people who really care for him). In general, Self-Sufficients are bright, overly responsible, overachieving, self-motivated, self-starting, somewhat perfectionist, often workaholic, wonderful people. We tend to become expert jugglers, orchestrating projects the size of the UN, balancing a baby on one knee while closing a lease on the Taj Mahal or managing the installation of a major software package while chaperoning a weeklong Boy Scout outing, all by ourselves. We are excellent employees, always pulling our weight plus a little more, typically performing way above average—what's to complain about? We are wonderful!

Of course, that's until the flames at each end of the candle meet in the middle and we join the ranks of the burned-out.

Q: If people can't really do or learn everything all by themselves and Self-Sufficients can't bring themselves to ask for help, how do they get the assistance they need?

A: Most Self-Sufficients will admit to allowing for a few legal loopholes in defining what it means to ask for help. Some examples are:

- It's not asking for help if we pay for the service, as in professional help.
- It's not asking for help if we learn the information in a class, read it in a book, or observe it by studying human nature.
- It's not asking for help if someone suggests a solution to a problem without our having to ask.

Cardinal guidelines like these allow the Self-Sufficient the option of attending as many classes and reading as many self-help books as he wants to without feeling like he is imposing or dependent upon or obligated to anyone. He can hire a service provider to assist him in reaching a goal, and it's considered a business transaction not a request for help. And, like the guy in the commercial who is eavesdropping on the stock market conversation at the next table at a restaurant, it's not asking for help if the information is just floating in the air and one *happens* to overhear.

Q: If living as a Self-Sufficient is so limiting and stressful, why would anyone adopt or choose to continue living this type of lifestyle?

A: We all know that when a behavior is detrimental to a person's well-being and she does it anyway, there's got to be some kind of payoff that keeps her tied to it. It's the "economy" of perceived pros and cons, costs and benefits, price tags and payoffs that underlies most human behavior. We've already mentioned many of these, but let's review the economics of Self-Sufficiency Syndrome shown in Figure 2.1.

Do you have difficulty analyzing yourself and your own behavior? I do. As a Self-Sufficient, I learn so much more from dropping back and becoming an observer of others. Not a bad way to learn—and it would work well at this point as we parse apart these pros and cons of severe self-sufficiency.

Think of a couple of people you know who look like they have it all together. Maybe they are the envy of many—others aspire to be just like them. They project a message to the world that they are in control and confident. Productivity is their priority. Do you notice them asking for help in tight places? Or do they always seem to manage everything all by themselves? How do they get it all done? Where do they get all that knowledge, drive, and persistence? What are the benefits that keep them so darn motivated? Why can't I do that?

The Economics of Self-Sufficiency Syndrome

Payoffs	Price Tags
Singular Control	No sense of belonging
	No help
	No objective feedback
	No team-building skills
	No backup support
	Mistrust
Approval and Admiration	No acknowledgment of needs
	No disclosure of needs
	No meeting of needs
Career Enhancement	Stress, fatigue, or illness from excessive responsibility
	Neglect or loss of primary relationships
Self-Confidence	Self-definition dependent upon most recent accomplishment
	Unrealistic standards and expectations
Minimal Obligations	Disconnection and isolation
	No reciprocity or "web of exchange"
No-Fault Reputation	Constant vigilance
	Fear of failure
	No opportunity for vulnerability
	No unconditional acceptance

Figure 2.1 The Economics of Self-Sufficiency Syndrome

Payoffs Versus Price Tags
for the Self-Sufficient

Payoff: Singular Control

Like an orchestra director, the Self-Sufficient gets up every morn-ing, baton in hand, ready to direct with poise and forethought everything and everyone who crosses her path. Rarely ruffled, she exudes confidence. People feel secure just being around her. Because she is so self-directed and well informed, she is the person people go to for answers. And if she doesn't have them, she'll get them—even if she has to take a hiatus behind the wall to do a quick check on the Internet.

She prefers to be given a task, left alone to design a strategy to ensure the desired outcome, and then be allowed to work on her own to get the job done—often with results surpassing expecta-tions. When this all works out, it's a process immensely gratifying to the Self-Sufficient. No interference, no conflicting viewpoints, no need to delegate . . . which is good, because if you'll watch close-ly, she can't. Delegate, that is. You see, to rely on someone else would mean giving up a portion of control, which might impact the outcome, which makes a Self-Sufficient sweat at the thought. If she's honest, she'd admit that she assumes the results of delegat-ing will be negative—in other words, other people will mess her thing up! It's interesting how anxious she is about other cooks in the kitchen—is she conceited, narcissistic, and full of herself? No, not usually. She is typically gracious in demeanor and consumed with work that, in the end, is of great benefit to others. No, she's not arrogant as much as she is afraid. *Really* afraid.

Her self-esteem is so tied to her performance, she dare not loosen even a pinkie on her grip of the project or task. God forbid, if she were to delegate and things went south, how would that reflect upon her? And even if things turned out okay, she can't really take credit for doing it all by herself, can she? Then the potential for gratification plunges, and that gratification is a key payoff if you're a Self-Sufficient. In other words, she prefers to have her name *alone* on the sign-off sheet. Singular control.

Price Tags for Singular Control

No Sense of Belonging This is the most astronomical price Self-Sufficients pay for looking like they have it all together—that they are invincible. As they give and give, helping others at every turn, they pray that it will buy them membership into the club without having to pay at the door with their vulnerability. But in spite of living an altruistic life, the Self-Sufficient feels like they're on the outside looking in. As we will see, the secret password to the club is give *and* take.

No Help Self-Sufficients are only human and when they go behind their wall where no one else can see, they can feel overwhelmed with what they've undertaken. They are frequently fending off a wave of private panic. Help, *real* help, sounds luxurious and perhaps tempting to reach out for—but no, that would defeat the whole purpose of why they do what they do, the way they do it. Asking for help would mean that they had failed even if the project succeeded. Nope, no help in sight for Self-Sufficients—by their own definition, they are not eligible.

No Objective Feedback This is pretty costly to give up. Objective feedback helps keep us on track when we aren't reading the road signs very well. It reminds me of that fairy tale, "The Emperor's New Clothes." Here we have a guy so sure that his perspective represents reality that he parades the streets of his kingdom stark naked, convinced of his belief that he is clothed in the finest of fabrics. Now *that* gentleman could have used some objective feedback!

A segment of an *Oprah* show about weight loss that aired when she was coming down from one of her all-time high weights comes to mind. They showed her and a close-knit group of friends and colleagues at her company who were exercising and working on weight loss together. Oprah talked about how when your weight fluctuates as hers has, you can lose an accurate visual perception of what size you are. She said when she looked at pictures of herself at her high weight, she was somewhat shocked—she had no real idea how much her size had gone up. "Why didn't you tell me?" she asked her friends, to which they replied, "We thought you knew." Understandable. Who would even think that this in-charge, self-directed icon of a successful woman would need (or appreciate) that kind of feedback?

No Team-Building Skills This is a no-brainer. If you're doing it all, all by yourself, who needs a team? You are the team, although it may feel more like a master/servant relationship when your drive to perform is always cracking the whip for you to do more and do it better. With team-building skills becoming increasingly necessary in the current and future business arena, the Self-Sufficient can come up short by not practicing the give-and-take of collaboration and mutual goal-setting with reliable colleagues and cohorts. Is there some risk involved? Sure, there is always the possibility that human error might play a role in the outcome, but when does he step back to allow others to make their own mistakes and have the opportunity to learn new skills? Has he ever considered that his need to exercise his strengths might be hindering those around him from having a chance to grow?

No Backup Support To stay in singular control means you are it! You had better have a Plan B and C . . . and D (just in case) because if you get too sick to crawl out of bed, or the roof caves in, what are you going to do? Not ask for help, of course—until it reaches the point of the ridiculous, and even then it would be great if someone would just read your mind and step up without your having to ask. Even though you jump at the chance to provide backup support for others, you have no safety net, no backup team, no cavalry to call when you are down for the count.

Mistrust A dyed-in-the-wool Self-Sufficient is pretty much bankrupt when it comes to trust. There are reasons. Stuff happened. They would say, "Been there, done that, didn't work out well." They, of course, would never let anyone know they didn't trust them—no, that might hurt their feelings and Self-Sufficients don't want to do that. So, they just stay out of situations where they would even have to trust anyone.

Angela wrote in one of my surveys, "I've discovered I am nearly incapable of accepting help except if I'm paying for it. My therapist nearly fell out of his chair when I told him I don't trust my friends to do certain things like meet me at the airport, or rescue me when my car is stranded, much less drive me home from the hospital after outpatient surgery. It is an incredibly lonely state to be in." The consequences of her inability to trust is one of the most significant losses the Self-Sufficient has to accept to be able to maintain singular control. So significant, that we'll examine the trust issue some more in a bit.

Payoff: Approval and Admiration

We've already touched on how much our culture approves of self-sufficiency. The profile of a person who has it all together, never needs anyone else, can take on more, accomplish more, and never cry "help" is set as the standard to be admired and attained. This person is sought and applauded in our business, social, and political institutions, and in the media. We love the rags-to-riches stories that fuel our free economy. We applaud those who make it against all odds. They are our heroes—and indeed, we should give credit where credit is due. For the Self-Sufficient, this kind of credit, applause, and approval is essential to his sense of well-being, so it's a huge payoff for him to do what it takes to stay in the circle of approval in his personal and professional life, and in society in general. How much does this cost?

Price Tags for Approval and Admiration

No Acknowledgment of Needs If you flip the coin of admiration for self-sufficient behavior, you'll see that our society equally abhors neediness. To be needy implies something close to a character flaw. That's why when we ask you in polite chitchat, "Hi, how are you doing?" we hope you understand that your line is, "I'm fine, thanks," no matter if you are or not. If your circumstances have taken a real turn for the worse, you're allowed to say, "Oh, I'm doing okay," which of course means that you're not okay. And if you should be so self-disclosing as to say, "Oh, I'm getting by, I guess," then you've gotten as close to admitting that your day, week, or life is currently going down the toilet as we want to know about. Whatever you do, don't say that you need something, because that makes us feel like we have to do something about it, which makes us feel uncomfortable. We would all appreciate it if you would just say you're fine and stay in denial like the rest of us. The Self-Sufficient has no trouble with this request since he decided a long time ago that the only reliable place to look if he needs something is in the mirror.

No Disclosure of Needs "My family measures success by how self-sufficient you act, so they are the last ones I'd let know that I am having real problems." This survey respondent is paying a high price for his family's approval, agreed?

Or what about the TV anchor who wrote me about her severe self-sufficient behavior to maintain her competitiveness in her field. She wanted to be the best, so every time anyone even commented about her voice, image, projection, etc., she'd run out and get a coach behind the scenes. She spent a fortune on lessons she could have gotten from those on the set—but the price she might have paid for that kind of disclosure might cost her too much in approval and admiration.

No Meeting of Needs When needs don't get acknowledged or disclosed, they rarely get met. That's the high price we pay for the approval we get as stoic Self-Sufficients. Here's a story I received from Meagan, along those lines:

"When I came home after major surgery, a family member came to stay with me and help me care for my family—a husband, a six-month-old baby, and a two-year-old. The family member left after two days 'because you're doing so well on your own' and didn't feel like I needed her to stay any more. I was doing tasks beyond my doctor's instructions. I was devastated when this person left but years later realized the reason: I couldn't graciously accept help, so I gave her the sense that she wasn't needed. Of course, the truth was I did need help, I wanted it, but I just couldn't accept it."

Payoff: Career Enhancement

Since Self-Sufficients put such an emphasis on their personal productivity, what corporation or organization wouldn't want them?

And since they take care of themselves, they're low maintenance too. High producers with low-maintenance needs—does it get much better than that? Throw in the added bonus that Self-Sufficients are willing to take care of everyone else, giving advice and assistance to anyone who knocks on their door, and it's clear that an employer typically finds a "value" when hiring one of them. These extreme characteristics actually give them an edge in the competitive, corporate environment. (The weakness that they are inevitably asked to reveal in a job interview usually is that they tend to be a perfectionist and very detail-oriented. They sometimes set the expectations of what they can achieve in a given time period a little bit too high.) The perks for being severely self-sufficient are particularly appealing for women who are competing for men's jobs, and they know to avoid any appearance of feminine dependency or vulnerability in the workplace if they want to get ahead.

Price Tags for Career Enhancement
Stress, Fatigue, or Illness from Excessive Responsibility The problem with promising a lot is that you have to pay the piper— and pay, and pay, and pay. The price tags for the payoff in a Self-Sufficient's career can be stress, fatigue, and illness. Although we are more comfortable in denial, in our lucid moments we know that marshaling the resources and skills to do everything all by ourselves is impossible.

No one was hardwired to do it all, and even when there are social accolades and admiration, the stress on body, mind, and soul can be too much. Always raising the bar on the quality of our achievements creates the kind of stress and fatigue that can shift our gears into panic position, drive us down heart attack alley, or knock at the door of complete burnout. Not surprisingly, 80 percent of all doctor's visits are related to stress. Wonder how many of those patients are Self-Sufficients, trying to maintain their status quo?

Neglect or Loss of Primary Relationships We Self-Sufficients often sabotage our close relationships because we:

- are all about accomplishment—we often spend so much time at work or focused on work that relationships dry up from neglect
- don't ask for what we need—our partner has to guess or give up
- give but don't realize that it's in the taking that we become close in our relationships
- take on too much responsibility in a relationship and have unrealistic expectations for ourselves

Dan's Story

Dan grew up in a family where the husband took care of everyone and everything. He didn't have a good role model for partnering. When he met Jane and they married, after a while she began to feel "left out." She never knew how much money they had or whether Dan was even doing well at his job. She tried to take over the responsibility of home repairs, but Dan would have none of that. He came home at lunch to meet repair people. After several years had passed, Jane realized that she didn't even know Dan, that he had an impenetrable shell that no amount of caring could penetrate. She asked him to see a counselor. Because he loved Jane, Dan agreed and came to learn that his attitude had cheated them both out of the opportunity to become close and share who they really were. After several months, Dan had made so much progress, he sat down with Jane and shared all their financial information—a huge step for him. Little by little, they worked their way through it, and for their next anniversary Dan gave Jane a Superman cape with a note saying he "was turning it in."

Payoff: Self-Confidence

One of the obvious payoffs of performing well is the inevitable sense of self-confidence that follows. This Self-Sufficient wrote it simply and best: "It makes me feel really good about myself that I can accomplish so much without any help." Achieving mastery of skills is gratifying and validating; receiving accolades for the work that results from using those skills can't help but build self-confidence and reinforce the drive to do more. This is all well and good—but is self-confidence the same as self-esteem? One distinction to consider is that the former is built on what one does, the latter on what one is. Obviously, they overlap, as what we do feeds into who we are and vice versa, but still it's a question worth considering and returning to later.

Price Tags for Self-Confidence
Self-Definition Dependent Upon Most Recent Accomplishment
For a Self-Sufficient, there's not much middle ground when it comes to self-definition. He sees himself in black and white; he's either competent or incompetent, a loser or a winner, a failure or a success. And the verdict on any given day is based on the outcome of his most recent endeavor. For the Self-Sufficient, the "job well done" satisfaction lasts only for a brief while. There is a fear that unless he maintains and increases his level of performance, he'll lose his worth, and worth is something he has to prove every day. That's why the typical Self-Sufficient's response to praise is, "Thanks, but that was nothing, anyone could have done that. I'm moving on to do XYZ now."

Unrealistic Standards and Expectations The problem about building her self-esteem on what she can accomplish is that there is no end to it. The last accomplishment was enough for then but not for now. That means her to-do list is always full, never fulfilled. There is no time to assess new skills gained—just onward and upward to the next accomplishment that has to be bigger, better, and more challenging. The expectations are huge and insatiable. And because they constantly escalate, it's easy to see how the Self-Sufficient is setting herself up for burnout.

Payoff: Minimal Obligations

Severe self-sufficiency offers a way to be in the world with no strings attached. People who have a history of getting all tangled up in their significant relationships see this as a very appealing payoff. It feels like freedom, but is it really?

Price Tags for Minimal Obligations
Disconnection and Isolation Janet cut her finger very badly. It was bleeding profusely, and her attempts to stop the bleeding weren't helping. She worked part-time for a plastic surgeon, so she called the office to see if he was there. When she found out that he was, she iced and wrapped her hand and drove herself, right hand up the entire trip, to his office downtown. Did she call for someone to take her? No. Did she even think about that? Probably not.

You understand by now that Self-Sufficients have a dilemma. Somewhere along the road of our development we learned that it's best to keep our needs to ourselves, that the whole transaction of give-and-take between human beings can be, at best, tricky and, at worst, heartbreaking. Don't get me wrong. We're not meek about what we want; we just prefer to bring our demands and expectations to one person, ourselves. Well, *prefer* is not completely accurate. If we were to dip down to our basic desires, we would admit that we ache to be able to call on others and count on them when we call. To rest in the comfort that others are there for us, that someone is attentive to our needs and will respond to our cries for help. But for some reason, we feel that counting on others is not a safe option and that, all in all, we'll fare better if we just take care of ourselves the best we can. We ignore our longing for belonging.

The Self-Sufficient's dilemma, then, is this: We *do* want to connect with others, and then again we don't. We *do* want to count on others, but then again we can't. We *do* want to be able to ask for help, but then again we won't. It's an ongoing, often subconscious, raging internal conflict. We often deny, ignore, or compartmentalize this conflict into a back closet of our psyche. It's just that smoke and heat keep escaping from under the door, cuing us that something really wrong is going on in there.

Many years ago when I was sharing a house with a college friend, my roommate went out for the evening, and I became violently ill. I was doubled over with stomach cramps and knew that it was serious. My roommate would have come running if she had known. There were friends I could have called if I didn't want to "disturb" my roommate's evening, and there were colleagues from my workplace who would have turned up in a minute. The idea of contacting any of them never even crossed my mind. My self-sufficient autopilot on full force, I got into my car and drove myself to the emergency room. I had to stop twice to let the pain pass, but I arrived, parked at the emergency entrance, and hobbled in. The diagnosis was food poisoning, and it was several days before they would let me leave the hospital.

No Reciprocity or "Web of Exchange" So, we see it's the give-and-take transaction that's the problem for the Self-Sufficient. She's got the *give* part down pat. She's all about giving in the ways that she can. That's why people love her as well as admire her accomplishments. It's the *take* part where she's inept. Receiving from another can arouse all kinds of anxious feelings so deep and confusing, they are hard to put into words. If the feelings could speak for themselves, maybe they would say:

- I can never give enough to deserve anything in return.
    Or
- I am afraid I will be disappointed with what I get in return, like what I want doesn't really matter to anyone else but me.
    Or
- If I take, I am obligated to give more, and I'm already giving as much as I can.
    Or
- If I let myself receive as well as give, then I'll lose my identity as "The Great Giver"—I would be nothing without that.
    Or
- I never learned how the give-and-take transaction works, and I'm lousy at it. If I start receiving, I may embarrass myself by taking too much or looking needy.
    Or
- If I receive as well as give, then I'll be admitting to myself that I'm not self-sufficient. I'll lose my bearings—I won't be able to justify the statement that keeps me going when all else fails: "I'm fine—I don't need anybody."

So the very thing we long for, healthy reciprocity in our relationships, is the very thing we can't allow ourselves to have. Why is that?

Payoff: No-Fault Reputation

"Throughout my working life," Lauren wrote me, "I have been rewarded for working harder, smarter, and faster than many others. I think these rewards have reinforced my do-it-yourself mentality. People in my inner circle find my self-sufficiency one of my most valuable qualities. However, I realize that this is probably slowing me down in accomplishing more of my vision for the future." Obviously, Lauren found a payoff for her self-sufficiency, and if that strength is just one of a spectrum of healthy adult character traits (like flexibility, resilience, open-mindedness, authenticity, and so on), then she should be in good shape. But she sounds like she may have some doubts about how well her degree of self-sufficiency is serving her goals and dreams. She appears to have earned a sterling reputation via her outstanding performance, but did she leave essential parts of herself behind to accomplish what she has? Now that she's established her profile as a do-it-yourselfer, is she limited by it? Does it take all of her energy to keep up her "harder, smarter, faster" image?

Price Tags for No-Fault Reputation

Constant Vigilance The concern is that once Lauren or any of us designs and establishes a presentation of ourselves to the world as extremely self-sufficient, we have the task of maintaining it. This translates into a never-let-your-hair-down, sleep-with-your-boots-on, always-check-your-side-mirror kind of vigilance that monitors our behavior, responses, and obligations. It gets really bad when we find ourselves competing with others to see if we can be the most self-sufficient, by taking on more than anyone else, with less help than anyone else. Wow, that kind of reputation can get expensive to your health, relationships, and sanity.

Fear of Failure The price tag for having a no-fault reputation is just that—you can't appear to have any faults. That's why the privacy wall we construct is so essential. It's where we go to reinvent ourselves depending on what the next situation calls for—or to work the bugs out of a new skill we are learning before going public. Believe me, this is a labor-intensive lifestyle—it takes a lot of work to be perfect. And even though we know it's impossible, we're going to keep trying for it.

Of course, if we know we absolutely cannot do something well (for instance, I'm not really cut out for cattle rustling), we won't even get in the vicinity of the endeavor. God forbid, someone might goad us into being a good sport and trying, and there, in front of the whole world or the few people who just might glance over, we could end up looking merely average—or worse!

All kidding aside, this fear-of-failure thing is no laughing matter to a Self-Sufficient. It provides enough negative incentive to make her early when everyone else is on time, keep him working after all the others have gone home, or keep them up when the sane folks have gone to bed, and to do this day after day, week after week, year after year. Whatever it takes to avoid failing—any other stress is preferable to the despair and worthlessness that a Self-Sufficient feels when he does his best and misses the mark. There are no small mistakes, no minor losses. That's the syndrome at its worst.

No Opportunity for Vulnerability We're afraid to fail because we are afraid mistakes make us unacceptable, worthy of rejection. We can't risk letting others in too close, inviting them behind the wall. That would never do.

This reminds me of back when I was dating a guy who was away at college. He wrote that he had taken up bowling and was hooked on it. He could hardly wait to get home so we could bowl together. Can you guess what I did? Me, who didn't know a strike from a spare? I got myself immediately to the local bowling alley, met my trainer (who, of course, was myself), and started rolling those gutter balls. I was awful but persistent, coming back again and again. Eventually, a few balls started making contact with the pins, which only strengthened my commitment to master this task.

By the time he came home, I could hold my own on the lanes. Of course, he was mystified and impressed, which was the whole point. I guess you could say this became my modus operandi, because I applied this same proactive, defensive stance to just about every challenge that came my way.

Remember Lauren's statement about the people in her "inner circle" seeing her self-sufficiency as her most valuable quality? I wonder if her perception of their opinion is completely accurate. They may be duly impressed by her performance, but do they feel a part of her life, do they feel the value of her needing them in any way, does she give them, as a dear friend asked of me, the dignity of helping *her* for a change?

And what about Lauren? Does she ever long for something deeper than praise and admiration, something that feels more like camaraderie and mutuality? A no-fault reputation may secure her seat up on that pedestal in her inner circle, but I wonder if she wouldn't find enormous comfort in climbing down and joining the others as just one of the gang around the campfire. Willing to be vulnerable in exchange for belonging—that's a very pricey transaction for the Self-Sufficient.

No Unconditional Acceptance This may be the most expensive price tag for a no-fault reputation, and for severe self-sufficiency overall. Acceptance is why we work so hard to do so much so well.

If we'd be honest, we would admit that we long to be accepted as we are, foibles and all. But we don't believe that's possible. Something about our experience reinforces our belief that we are only acceptable based on how we perform. So we crack the whip and hold ourselves to a higher standard of acceptability than we do most others.

The Self-Sufficient is a tough taskmaster over his own actions. He will typically admonish himself and berate his own mess-ups much more harshly than anyone else would. In response to a faux pas or oversight, it is not unusual to hear a Self-Sufficient call himself "Stupid!" or "Idiot!" under his breath, something he would rarely say about someone else making a similar mistake. Why is he so much more accepting of other people's mistakes than of his own? Is there something about him that makes him less acceptable than others— or that makes a mistake so much worse if he makes it rather than someone else? Did he just get a smaller length of slack when grace was being distributed to the human race, or what?

The Bottom Line

Okay, here we are at the end of the payoffs and price tags. If you remember when we began, I asked that you choose a couple of people that you think might be Self-Sufficients.

How did the people you chose compare to the prototypical Self-Sufficient we've described? Can you see evidence of the payoffs in their lives? The price tags are a bit harder to detect, but, sooner or later, hairline cracks begin to appear and widen in the strained façade of their privacy wall. Glimpses of the toll this lifestyle takes become more visible, until one day, you just might find this dear one with a head up against the cold marble of a rest-room wall, heart racing and palms sweating with a full-blown case of Self-Sufficiency Syndrome.

How can people trying to do everything so right find them-selves so overwhelmingly stuck in the far reaches of severe self-suf-ficiency? Keep reading.

CHAPTER THREE

The Different Kinds of
Self-Sufficients

The important thing is not to stop questioning.
Curiosity has its own reason for existing.
ALBERT EINSTEIN

So, what do we understand so far? We described the prototypical Self-Sufficient sitting way out on the edge of life controlled by a pattern of extreme, self-perpetuating behavior. Simply put, she's just plain stuck. Let's take a moment to look at the etiology of the syndrome. Where in the heck did the stimulus to become severely self-sufficient come from? When and why did she buy into behavior that's so unbalanced? How did she get stuck out on the end of that seesaw with no help in sight?

It appears that Self-Sufficiency Syndrome can originate from a variety of possible sources. For starters, many adopt this behavior from an influential role model or in response to crisis situations in their early years. We'll call this group the Inheritors.

The Inheritors

Jean, an upper-level manager in an international company, grew up in a home with a strict, dictatorial father. While interviewing her, she told me she didn't remember much real conversation in her child-hood home. She couldn't remember ever receiving praise from her parents or siblings. "The word love was never spoken. We were encouraged to stand on our own two feet and be self-sufficient." In a family of all girls, she became her father's favorite. From this tenuous position, she learned to suck it up and not complain about anything.

This caught up with her, however, in her adult years, when, no matter what she accomplished, she was aware that something was blocking her from experiencing happiness. "I knew there was something wrong, but I couldn't identify what it was." Still she kept herself to herself, trying to understand and solve her strug-gles all by herself—until finally she just couldn't. "I had success-fully isolated myself from everyone. I had to be self-sufficient even at figuring out what was wrong with me. Finally, I just got tired of feeling bad all the time. I started talking with people about it." She was amazed at the reaction. "I actually got praise for being vulnerable . . . the first time I got praise in my life. I had always hidden my vulnerabilities, but that just takes too much energy. I let go of that defensive wall around me that I thought was hiding my insecurities." Letting go and taking the risk to open up to trusted individuals paid off. "Finding happiness has been a diffi-cult process for me that took much longer than it needed to because, for so long, I would not seek help."

It's impossible to grow up in a home and not, in some ways, mimic our caretakers. Good, bad, or indifferent, they are our first and most influential role models, and what they say, how they act, and what they value becomes the baseline for our view of the world. How they see things (morals, ethics, values, prejudices) becomes "truth" to us, no questions asked. But then, as we move from childhood to adolescence, we do start questioning. "Why do they do that? What happens when they do? Is this what I want for myself? Do I really believe what they believe? How do I know if what they say is really the way things are?"

Without a lot of exposure to the outside world, it's difficult to assess role models, isn't it? And even if we dare, part of us isn't too keen on doing it. These early caretakers have been our "giants," those we look up to, and bringing them down at any juncture is difficult. Often, we reach middle age before we're fortified with enough maturity and life experience to challenge our early upbringing. Even then, we're probably not interested in going back to condemn or judge but to understand where we came from and whether we approve of what we're carrying forward to the next generation. We look back to gain insight on how to change our course, if need be, to improve the quality of our life and the lives that follow after us.

Ever heard the story about the ham pan? A bride cuts off the end of the ham each time she prepares it. Her new husband asks why. "Because my mother did," she says. The next time he's with his new mother-in-law, he asks her. "Because *my* mother did," she replies too. Luckily, his bride's grandmother comes to visit, allowing him to pursue the answer to the great mystery. "Nana, why do you cut the end off the ham each time before you cook it?" Her insightful answer? "Because my pan is too short for a whole ham."

That story made an impression on me. Often we get stuck in an autopilot way of living, replicating the values and patterns of early role models without much analysis. Since self-made independence is considered virtuous by our culture, why would we question or examine it? No reason to ask ourselves if "doing it all, all by myself" might be an extreme and unbalanced way to live. Our role models were obviously proud that they were able to stand on their own two feet and never have to ask for help. Why wouldn't we try to emulate them and perpetuate the principles of: "If you want it done right, do it yourself"; "Don't bother the neighbors"; or "You better learn to be self-sufficient—when the going gets rough, who else are you going to depend on?" When handed down from generation to generation, it can be hard to admit, or even see, the handicaps in a highly esteemed belief system—harder still to break from embedded patterns we have adopted from our role models, patterns leading to life as a one-man show, no supporting cast or crew required.

Most of us inherit the perspective of our parents or another prominent family caretaker, but perhaps your childhood role model for extreme self-sufficiency was a teacher, a coach, or an influential neighbor. For some of us, things were so chaotic at home, we went outside the family to find an alternative role model. Perhaps a Self-Sufficient filled the bill.

I remember a conversation I had a few years ago with psychologist Monica Ramirez Basco, author of *Never Good Enough*. Here's the gist of what she said: Awareness can be such a huge help in seeing our behavior and where it isn't serving us. When people who have unknowingly inherited severe self-sufficiency become aware of that fact, I think they will find it relatively easy to break out of the patterns.

The Islanders

"No man is an island" . . . or is he? Self-Sufficients often admit they feel alone in a crowd. They can plan an event, chair a meeting, host a party, even oversee "breaking the ice" among the guests, and never feel that they joined the gathering themselves. They facilitate connection for others and then stand alone, apart, more comfortable in the kitchen, in the corner, or behind a podium than in eyeball-to-eyeball interaction with the humans in attendance. Floating through life, emotionally unattached in a sea of familiar faces, we call these Self-Sufficients the Islanders.

Of course, some of us become Islanders just to cope—at least that's what I hear from former latchkey kids, foster children, or kids who became caretakers for an ill or addicted parent. When life hands us these kinds of challenges at such a tender age, learning to do everything all by yourself isn't so much a choice as it is a survival measure. And it *does* work to get us through, most of the time. However, like the best of medicines, there can be unwanted, long-term side effects. Feeling perpetually alone and emotionally unattached may be one of the residual side effects of childhood severe self-sufficiency that we carry into adulthood.

What else might play a role in creating an Islander? How about the contemporary reality that affects all of us: the speed of change. Think about it. Never before in the history of this planet have humans experienced so much consistent change as fast as the last five generations.

Diane, a speech-language pathologist who works with stroke patients, told me recently about her 101-year-old patient, who was sharp as a tack, recounting memories of helping her brothers crank up their first Model T automobile in 1912. Picture this lovely, articulate centenarian relaying stories of early twentieth-century events, as she sat with a cell phone in hand waiting for her granddaughter to call to send photos of the great-grandchildren and inform her when she would be flying in to see her that afternoon (from a distance it would have taken that Model T four days to travel!). That one scene gives us a glimpse of what we seldom grasp: the rate of technological change for us and our grandparents, parents, children, and grandchildren has become and will continue to be exponential. It's so fast, the full impact doesn't register. Like mice in a laboratory, it's hard to be the experiment and analyze, comprehend, and interpret the experiment at the same time.

What we do know is this. As our culture becomes more and more mobile, as we break away from families and friends to move every few years across state, region, and country, becoming increasingly self-sufficient is necessary. Going off on your own often means leaving everyone and everything familiar behind. Technology offers us stopgap methods to stay in touch, but I question whether these measures are enough to maintain a real sense of connection and belonging over time.

What is it about our culture that is escalating our separateness? I thought the other day, "You know, riding around in this car is like traveling in a socially sterile bubble. . . . I drive through the bank, pick up my cleaning, get my prescriptions, wash my car, and go to a drive-through for lunch or a latte, without having to interact with anyone." Remember when we used to develop casual, familiar relationships with the postal clerk, the druggist, the teller at the bank, the receptionist at the doctor's office? They became friends over time—people we trusted and counted on to help us in their areas of expertise. We weren't just customers, clients, or patients—we were people with names and families and individual histories and circumstances. We could ask for help, but we often didn't need to—these people typically knew what we needed before we could even ask.

Now we're talking to computerized voices when we call for customer service. We can comparison shop, order holiday gifts, check on missing orders, follow packages across country during delivery, and never interact with anyone other than an artificial voice. I used to joke in workshops that I was so polite, I never interrupted a computerized voice; my traditional Southern upbringing always kicks in, and I wait until the computer has finished its sentence.

With the support of advanced technologies, more people are leaving corporate employment to go off on their own. That's great—we need and applaud the entrepreneur, the independent contractor or consultant, the small-business owner who builds a vision, takes the risks, and works her dreams into reality. But until recently one still had to maintain some regular contact with others, entering their physical space, so to speak, to do business or to receive services (as in sales appointments, loan interviews, community projects, association meetings, and regular customer service calls).

Add to this trend the fact that, after the workday is done, more and more of us are going home alone. The current number of single dwellers in the United States, including individuals who are unmarried, divorced, widowed, or elderly, is approximately ten million and climbing.

All of this technological expediency, efficiency, and convenience—is it so we can have more time for relationships with the people we care about? That's what the ads promise, but let's be honest. In the real world, it's all about getting this done quicker so we can do more after that, increasing productivity both in our professional and personal lives. The ceaseless busyness fuels a growing sense of corporate isolation, so that the thing we most have in common is how little time we have for anything but work. Most of us are so busy, an e-mail might be the closest we come to a face-to-face conversation with a close friend or relative for months.

When I lived in Dallas, I occasionally picked up a Breakfast Jack when I had a 7:00 a.m. meeting. Once, very early, I was surprised to be one of the few in line, so I took the opportunity to actually talk to the person at the window where I was picking up my order. "What's going on?" I asked.

"Not much," he replied.

"Hey, you mean you all do two million transactions a day across the United States and nothing is happening?"

"Well, locally, we do seem to have an epidemic. People come through the drive-through line, order their breakfast, pay for it, and then just drive off, without picking it up."

"Do they come back?" I asked, curious.

"Sometimes, but not often."

"Why not? Do you think they're embarrassed?"

"Nah, I'll tell you what I think. Sometimes, I get to work and don't know how I got here. I'm concentrating on the fifty things I have to do before 10:00 A.M. I think these people are all so busy, I think they think they ate it!"

The Icons

The third type of Self-Sufficient is the Icon. This is the type of individual we put on a pedestal. Never needy, always together, helping everyone around him but never needing help himself—hey, what's not to look up to?

The Icon might well have inherited her behavior from a role model. "If it was good enough for them, then . . . " And they may have chosen an Islander career or lifestyle because it supports that success. But the Icons have special characteristics all their own. Ever heard the term trust issues? Well, Icons got 'em. Something in their experience early on impressed them with the fundamental belief that "the world is not a safe place—you cannot really trust others." If this perspective becomes entrenched, becoming severely self-sufficient becomes a way to diminish the risk of being hurt, disappointed, and, worst of all, abandoned. Although Icons are admired for their fierce independence, these individuals are conning themselves.

The Icon sees the benefits of staying severely self-sufficient to be worth their price. He cons himself into believing that staying in complete control and achieving his way to self-esteem will take care of any insecurities and empty places that remain under lock and key inside him. He will go on assuming too much responsibility, working too many hours, setting too many high goals, mentally driving himself on to the next trophy before the last one is on the shelf, all because, in the end, he needs to see himself as able to protect himself from failure—his own and that of anybody else associated with him. Often, even when a goal is reached, he's not really satisfied unless he feels that he did it or could have done it all by himself. To the Icon, sharing the limelight isn't much better than being in the dark.

The Icon sees these benefits as the solution to a deep-seated fear of being subject to the whims of others; avoiding vulnerability is worth any price, including all the disadvantages of severe self-sufficiency we discussed earlier. She cons herself into the mind-set that she's better off never depending on anyone, for if she never fully trusts, she cannot be disappointed; if she never fully leans, she cannot be let down; and if she only gives but never asks for help, she will never be obligated. The Icon will cling to her image of being totally capable, not granting herself any slack to benefit from the suggestions, support, or sympathy of others. Yes, it is an approach that keeps emotions neat and tidy—and people lonely.

So Which One Are You?

These three categories of the Self-Sufficiency Syndrome are not mutually exclusive. Someone might see himself in one, two, or all three categories. So let's get personal. How about you? To what degree do you feel that you are the only person you can trust, that you'd better do everything yourself so that it gets done correctly? Not at all? A little bit? Most of the time?

Granted, there are things I can't do one darn thing about. I can't change your history or your gene pool—I can't magically take away the fears you may have good reason to have. I can, however, help you pinpoint where you're stuck, no matter how you got there. I can suggest ways that you can move away from the extreme end of the bell-shaped curve, keeping all the benefits of being able to rely on yourself when you decide to—but also having permission to seek help, support, and (think of it!) companionship from others when you want to. Actually, the solutions are pretty simple. I didn't say easy, I said simple—simple to grasp and understand, *but* like any tweaking or adjustment of entrenched behavior, they will take effort. Of course, I'm not talking to wimps, am I? Not if you rate yourself in the severe zone of self-sufficiency.

Are you suffering from Self-Sufficiency Syndrome? If you're not sure, that's okay—there are some tools coming up to help you evaluate yourself. If you're honest, these exercises will help give you a better idea of whether your self-sufficient behavior is extreme. I'll keep using the seesaw as a visual to see how to move from being stuck out on the end toward the middle—a position of balance and more real control than you've probably ever experienced before.

CHAPTER FOUR

Assessing Your Level of Self-Sufficiency

Self-knowledge is the beginning of self-improvement.
SPANISH PROVERB

How many bells went off as you read the previous chapter? What did you identify with the most? How many defenses went up? The question is: just how self-sufficient are you?

There are countless variations of Self-Sufficients. There are probably as many causes, reactions, and experiences as there are individuals reading this. All I'm after is to let you know whether you need to put some new behaviors in place to get you into a more balanced place—one that will make your life more fulfilling and rewarding.

Exercises

I'm all for developing the mind and body, but I have to say, I don't like exercises. We Self-Sufficients tend to be so competitive, we look at the score, look at the points we scored low on, and hold them in disdain forever more. We get all wrapped up in how we relate relative to others, rather than the benefits we can get just by participating. If that sounds like you, let me clarify that these exercises are just for you to learn more about yourself.

The emphasis is on helping you get some objectivity about your behavior. Because, when it comes right down to it, you know yourself better than anyone—and you only stand to gain by assessing where you really are, what you want to do about it, and what you have to work with, right?

I also want to share some feedback from questionnaires and surveys. In workshops, online, and by mail, I have conducted a number of different surveys to give me information. I received some incredible comments and insights that I hope will help you in this process. In fact, let's start with some of these.

In an online survey conducted some two years before the writing of this book, here are some questions I asked:

1. Are you burned out because you do everything all by yourself?
2. Did doing everything all by yourself come from a family rule or example?
3. Is there something you fear about asking for help?
4. If you do ask for help, how did you learn to ask?

Here's some input from that survey.

- 64 percent said yes to being burned out.
- 60 percent said yes to a family example.

Fears included:

- Looking stupid; not viewed as competent.
- I feel that if I put myself out in the world, then I will find out I am not as special and clever as I thought I was."

- People tend to treat you like an idiot because you don't know everything they know.
- There's always the fear of refusal. And what do you say to the person . . . friend, family, or other when they have not agreed to help?
- Looking weak; other people losing confidence in me; losing the illusion (sense of security) that I can handle anything.
- Someone taking over and doing the whole thing for me; others taking credit for all of the work.
- I'll owe somebody and won't be happy until I pay it back.
- The task not being completed the way I would like it to be.
- Feeling of being subordinate to others.
- That no one can do the task as well as I can.
- I've learned that the only person I can really count on is myself. I'm always there for me.
- That people will think less of me if I do ask for help.
- Independence is a huge thing to me and having to rely on another person can be a blow to my confidence.
- I fear that I will impose on someone. My mother taught me to never bother anyone else with something you can do for yourself.
- Some part of me wants everyone to know that I can do it all."
- It stems from fearing that people will view me as weak, which is a silly thing, but I think it's a learned trait. The less often you ask for help, the harder it is to ask—kind of a self-fulfilling prophecy.
- Around the house, I really enjoy being self-sufficient and find it a strength. I'll tackle just about any repair job: replace a

light switch, connect the gas dryer, plant a big tree. At work, however, I feel somehow driven to do it all and always have too much on my plate. I try really hard to delegate, but responsibilities somehow find their way back to me.

- I thrive on the recognition from accomplishing a task or doing something well. If you ask for help, then some of that recognition is taken away from you.
- It feels as though I'm surrendering some of my power and giving it to them."

Action Steps

1. So, did you read anything you agree with?
2. Do you have similar fears?
3. Make a list for yourself. Because when we get to the chapters on ACT and the Fulcrum, you'll be able to challenge and change your fears and the beliefs that support them.
4. Is it a help to realize others feel the very same way? That you're not alone?

Here's a typical story from one of my surveys. Patty wrote: "My husband mimics our middle child by saying 'I do it!' to me every time I try to do something by myself that he thinks I need his help to do. The story is that our middle child was very independent as a toddler and always wanted to try things himself, so he would tell us 'I do it!' when we tried to peel a banana for him or tie his shoes, or any other task he wanted to try by himself. I tend to tackle things I should ask for help doing because I was taught to not bother the neighbors."

Your Turn

The following exercises are designed to stimulate your thinking, explore patterns in your behavior, and perhaps confirm some instinctive feelings. Questions you may be asking are:

- How can I tell if I'm too self-sufficient?
- Do I have self-defeating behaviors?
- What will I learn and what can I do with the results?

Remember Your Strengths

First, you'll need help identifying and appreciating your *strengths*. Put a check beside each strength that you can claim:

My friends/coworkers/family members praise me for my:

_____ Self-discipline
_____ Self-determination
_____ Self-motivation
_____ Resilience
_____ Persistence; tenacity
_____ Resourcefulness
_____ Ability to multitask
_____ Other _____

Each of these strengths has helped you in the past as you've mastered self-sufficiency. They will be there for you again as you undertake a new challenge. This is not about learning something new. It's a relearning process.

The Circling Exercise

This exercise will enable you to see just how balanced or extreme your self-sufficiency may be. Take your time to browse through both Lists A and B in Figure 4.1. Which characteristics best describe your life? If you're not sure, think about how your closest friend would describe you. Circle any characteristic that is true of you, whether it is found in A or B. Count the number of items circled in List A and then List B. List A represents the extreme

The Circling Exercise

List A	List B
Driven	Persevering
Controlling	Cooperative
Prefer competing against others	Open to collaborating with others
Demand perfection	Accept imperfections
Rigid	Flexible
Reluctant to ask for help	Willing to ask for help
Afraid to fail	Learn from mistakes
Assume total responsibility	Share responsibility and delegate
Don't deserve help	Entitled to receive help
Must be the giver	Balance giving and taking
Secretly feel insecure	Feel adequate and confident
Feel alone and separate	Feel connected and supported

Figure 4.1: The Circling Exercise

behavior of a Self-Sufficient, and List B represents the balance of being a Sufficient-Self. (You'll hear a lot more about the Sufficient-Self later.) If most of your circled characteristics are in List A, this indicates that you exhibit extreme or severe self-sufficiency. If there is a mix of the two lists, as long as there are items circled in List A, you'll want to follow many of the solutions we offer later. In our self-serve society, it's too easy to be pulled to the other side. If most of your circled items are from List B, then you may want to look at the path you took to get there and share it with others.

True or False

In the blank before each statement, answer true or false.

_____ 1. Once I accept help from someone, it creates a debt I have to repay.

_____ 2. At this moment, I can recall asking someone for help within the last month.

_____ 3. It's not asking for help if I pay for it—as in taking a workshop, seeing a counselor, or buying a book.

_____ 4. After fouling something up, I can usually laugh at myself with acceptance and amusement.

_____ 5. Having to ask for help to understand something would mean I'm not smart enough to figure it out on my own.

_____ 6. Nine times out of ten, I feel a job will only get done right if I do it myself.

_____ 7. I'm more likely to call tech support at the first sign of computer problems; it's just not worth the hassle of trying to read the manual.

_____ 8. I am less anxious when I am in the position to control events, things, and people.

_____ 9. I get more satisfaction when I am collaborating with others rather than competing with them to reach a goal.

_____ 10. When things get out of control, I usually don't panic—I can remain calm, adjust my expectations, and get help when I need it.

How did you do? Statements 1, 3, 5, 6, and 8 would be answered true by a Self-Sufficient, whereas statements 2, 4, 7, 9, and 10 would be answered false. If you answered 8 out of these 10 statements in this way, it's a strong indication that you are severely self-sufficient. If you answered 6 out of 10 as a Self-Sufficient would, you are on the borderline. From the results of both exercises above, your degree of self-sufficiency should be apparent.

On a Scale of 1 to 5

Below are statements made by Self-Sufficients. Rate yourself on a scale of 1 to 5 (1 = very rarely; 5 = more often than not). Since each of these is written by someone exhibiting Self-Sufficiency Syndrome, you'll be able to see where you fall on the spectrum.

_____ 1. I will do my own job without help and then jump in and help everyone else.

_____ 2. If someone talks about a problem, no matter what it is, I usually have some advice.

_____ 3. I get very nervous when someone tries to help me; I feel like I'm under a spotlight.

_____ 4. I worry after I've finished something; maybe I didn't do it as well as I could have.

_____ 5. I feel mild to severe anxiety most of the time because I feel that it's all up to me.

_____ 6. When I make a mistake, it's very hard to shake it off, so I work doubly hard not to make any.

_____ 7. No one offers to help me because I look like I know how to do everything; I can bluff my way through anything.

_____ 8. I focus on the place where I get the most approval, so work has been it. If you let me, I'll work sixteen hours a day and never take a vacation.

_____ 9. If I can't do something well, I just don't do it. If I feel pressured, I learn how when no one is around.

_____ 10. I rarely feel pleased with an outcome.

_____ 11. I don't delegate because if someone else did a good job, where would I be?

_____ 12. I can get along just fine all by myself.

_____ 13. I am the supreme juggler. I can get more done in a day than most people can in three.

_____ 14. I am often tired from doing it all.

_____ 15. I always seem to be the one who gets assigned another job.

_____ 16. If I'm not an expert at almost everything, I can't feel good about myself.

Now, count up the number of statements that you checked, and then divide 16 into that number. This will give you your average. You may even get a fraction but that's okay. If over half, take it to the next number and if under, take it to the lower number. An average of

1 or 2 will indicate your balanced self-sufficiency. An average of 3 may demonstrate a tendency to be too self-sufficient. An average of 4 or 5 is self-explanatory.

Evaluation Time: What's Your Diagnosis?

Okay, what do you think now? I hope these exercises were helpful in taking a look at yourself and your behaviors in life. It's so difficult to see ourselves without something or someone to mirror back what we're doing.

How severely self-sufficient are you? After all the exercises, on a scale of 1 to 5, where would you put yourself? Look back at each exercise. If you had just a few in the severe self-sufficiency category, then you may be balanced in your self-sufficiency. If you were midline, then look through the solutions and apply the ones you need. If severe, please read the whole book, work the solutions, and work with others.

Just let it help you decide if it's not working for you anymore. Take all the time you need on this section. This investigation can be critical.

- Write down what you found.
- What's your first step?
- Buck up your courage to share this knowledge with a best friend or two.

Once the truth is spoken, it's very difficult to retract—it pushes us forward to let another human being in on what's going on. We call it *vulnerability*.

CHAPTER FIVE

Ready, Willing, and Able:
Preparing for Change

At first people refuse to believe that a strange new thing
can be done, then they begin to hope it can be done,
then they see it can be done—then it was done,
and all the world wonders why it was
not done centuries ago.
FRANCES HODGSON BURNETT

Question

Okay! I can see that being a Self-Sufficient hasn't been as fulfilling as it could have been. So, let's say that I am open to
making a few minor adjustments to my way of living. Why do I
need to read this chapter?

Answer

Thanks for that question! We've acknowledged that our past
behavior has been to excel at anything we accomplish and we avoid
those things we can't. If I can make you familiar with this process
of change, I know you'll excel! That's what this chapter does. It
talks you though all the pitfalls and preparation. It describes the

change process—how to prepare—what to do. Once you're ready, we explore your willingness. Then open to change, I'll provide the solutions in later chapters, enabling you to be successful.

Ready to Redesign Your Comfort Zone?

"Time out"—that's what we've come to use as punishment for little kids. No wonder—standing in the corner, isolated, looking at the walls where they meet, being told to *think* about what we did—what card-carrying Self-Sufficient wouldn't consider that punishing? Who wants to reflect? We're much too busy for introspection. We've got deadlines to meet, projects to finish. . . . Time out is not an option.

Of course, it *is* convenient to have our excessive busyness to justify the fact that we really prefer not to reflect, not to examine all the feelings we pushed into that corner and hoped would just magically go away. Anyway, we're kind of comfortable with the setup the way things are—we might be open to rearranging a few pieces of furniture, but let's not get radical and change the whole decor! We've established a comfort zone, and yes, it may be flawed and in need of some repair, but it's ours and it's familiar and, well, we'd just as soon let it be. We've become comfortable with the way we do things and, bottom line, it just feels safer than any other way.

What we're saying is that inside the comfort zone we build for ourselves, we practice methods of doing things that seem to work for us, based on past experience. To stay comfortable, we've held on to those habits. Like an old pair of slippers, we pull out these well-worn, automatic methods and habits and apply them to every new situation—those fuzzy, bunny flip-flops become the footwear of choice for every occasion.

Jamie McKenzie, Ed.D., explains it this way:

Unfortunately, life in the comfort zone is addictive for many. Once we have tasted the security and predictability of life in the comfort zone, our desire for comfort often seems to grow and we require even larger doses to maintain equilibrium. We begin to confuse the comfort zone and the feelings it generates with normality—the "way it's spozed to be." Comfort is normal, we feel. Discomfort is abnormal. Risk is an enemy because it threatens disruption.

All right. I admit that's nailed it. Makes perfect sense to me. How about you?

Can't we make these new adjustments *within* the confines of our good old normal comfort zones? We really really like those old slippers.

No matter how comfortable we may be, there is no advancement or growth unless we stretch the boundaries. "Thinking outside the box" has become a common approach to creativity. Will changing our extreme patterns of self-sufficiency challenge us to think outside the box of our comfort zones? Absolutely! What will our next comfort zones look like?

Well, we'll need a blueprint. Getting ready, being willing, and becoming able to envision, design, and implement that blueprint will facilitate the change. Our goal will be to develop ourselves to the point that our next comfort zone will be a showplace featuring more balance, stability, and flexibility. Can we get comfortable with that?

Question: How does my comfort zone affect others?

Answer: Now you're thinking. If we're to balance our accomplishments with our relationships, let's consider what changes might do to our important relationships. As we get ourselves ready, it's important to understand that if we change, we'll be asking others to change *their* comfort zones, too.

I remember the impact that psychologist, author, and lecturer John Bradshaw had on my thinking back in the 1980s when he demonstrated this point with a mobile he used.

Maybe you saw him on PBS and remember it. The mobile consisted of disks representing family members. As Bradshaw would move one piece on the mobile, each family piece would move; it was impossible to move one without affecting all. It was a profound lesson for me.

People Who Need People

Our behaviors and our boundaries that we set control how others respond to us. This sets up a comfort zone with each person who interacts with us, and when we change that dynamic in any way, we automatically change their comfort level too. Some find this very disconcerting. You awake one fine morning and ask your husband to get the vase from the top shelf. He's overcome. He has lived for this moment but, unprepared for the shock, decides that you have a terminal illness that has incapacitated you—for given his experience, there could be no other logical explanation.

Like us, some of those around us don't like having change "sprung" on them by someone else either. Let's say, one day you've decided to change your ways and give notice to others in your world that you won't be doing everything for them anymore. Who'll cover the gap? Now, you realize that some people in your life have become very dependent on your being responsible for them. They may have forgotten how to do many jobs you've been doing. Even worse, they may never have had the chance to learn. Maybe they even expressed a desire to learn, but after a while it became easier to just let go and let you do it all, all by yourself. I think Dr. Murray Bowens's label of "overfunctioner" might well apply here.

Prepare to get strong reactions when you announce you're changing horses in midstream. In order to preserve their comfort zone, you can be sure some will attempt to persuade you to go back to the old ways. You're already dealing with your own internal struggles to change and now you will have the added pressure of others subtly or overtly trying to get you to return to the status quo. No doubt about it, this can make changing so overwhelmingly difficult, it's tempting to throw in the towel.

But don't. Instead think about how you'll prepare for this. How will you get those around you ready to support you in these changes rather than fight you at every turn to pull you back? This will be critical.

Action Steps

1. *Share with a close relationship what you'd like to change.* This will be difficult because you'll feel vulnerable. It'll be a form of asking for help. Some of us have never shared this vulnerability because we don't want it thrown in our faces later.

   If we can't trust our closest relationships to support us in this important change, let's seek out others who are ready to make some changes too.
2. *Communication will be the secret to success.* I learned this from a workshop participant who evaluated herself as a Self-Sufficient after taking the assessment questionnaire.

After the workshop, she asked to take one home to her sixteen-year-old daughter. Later, I got a letter from her saying that she'd told her daughter about the workshop and asked her an important question, "Do I act like I don't need anyone else?" It only took about 10 seconds for her daughter to respond that, yes, she *did* act like she did-n't need anyone. The kicker is that then her daughter took the questionnaire and scored even higher than Mom. "What this did for us is to start a meaningful conversation," she wrote.

She took the initiative to communicate—to ask the important question and be open for the answer. The only way the significant others in your life will know how much you need their support will be if you communicate how important making these changes is to you. When they understand that, then you can appeal for flexibility and negotiate a plan that keeps you on track without turning their world upside down.

Boil, Boil, Toil, and Trouble

Have you heard that story about the frog in boiling water? It's a great story to give you some perspective. A frog is put into boiling water and jumps out—he's no fool. But when put into cold water and the temperature raised gradually, the frog boils—and I sub-mit to you that that's exactly what's happening to many of us.

We become conditioned to our situation. After all, most of us pride ourselves on the ability to handle anything life throws our way—better than anyone else. Why would we possibly have to ask for help and break our record? What an absurd idea! We've become so conditioned to doing more, accomplishing more, that we wouldn't be the same without it. In fact, we usually operate better when we're in hot water.

Many of us have become quite skilled at crisis. Besides, those crisis skills have come in handy. While others are panicking, we're able to step into the breach and bring order out of chaos. What a skill for anyone in corporate America today! Even the culture says it's wonderful, and so we proceed, feeling we're on the right track, never stopping to wonder how extremist our behavior is.

"What we resist persists." That quote says it all. Do you notice how life keeps throwing you the same lessons to learn? Since you're on autopilot, there's no time to look at the issue—so if life has decided this is an important lesson, then the tests will have to continue to get tougher each time to get your full attention. But what do we like the most? A challenge, so we can show off our skills that we do better than anyone else.

No wonder we don't feel the water heating up. We've adapted to the norm of high temperature, which means that we are oblivious as our situation gets more complex, more serious, more overwhelming each time, not even hearing that common sense voice within us screaming, "Hey, don't you get it? How hard would it be to get out of hot water and just ask for some help?" Writing these words, I can feel the water around me, getting hotter, harder to handle, bringing waves of stress and sleepless nights.

——— ———

As I told you in Chapter Two, I began to have panic attacks. For you, it might be another more serious illness brought on by all the stress. Whatever it takes to heat the water to make you cry uncle and start to address the priorities that you've been running from—you can count on life to provide that learning opportunity for you.

We are smart, gifted people with scads of skills and strengths. Otherwise, we couldn't have pulled this off as long as we have. If we can allow ourselves a "time-out" to assess how really close we are to burnout, we might decide to get out of that boiling pot and work at change.

Dr. Bridges's Model for Change

Dr. William Bridges, industrial psychologist and a leading guru on the topic of change wrote an outstanding book entitled *Transitions*. I can't begin to count the numbers of outplaced workers I've counseled who have drawn encouragement and direction from this work. In it, he explains that every transition has an ending and a beginning.

For example, the end of being overweight is the beginning of being sleek and slim. For us it would be the end of being so self-sufficient and the beginning of asking for help. However, Bridges also tells us that human beings can't make that transition so quickly. We need some time and space in between. Dr. Bridges calls it "the neutral zone."

In order to get ready, to be willing to change, and to be able to make it happen, let's visit each stage along the way.

The Ending

Webster's defines *ending* as the last part or finish. The action, situation, relationship, position, or condition is over. The ending requires us to admit to ourselves that there is a loss involved. We have terminated actions, feelings, and commitments and closed our hearts and minds to any further participation. The next day we move on.

Were it that easy. Even on wonderful, happy occasions where a change is taking place, there's a feeling of loss associated with the ending.

The first day my children went to school, I was so excited— their new clothes, the lunch box, them looking so grown-up. And that's the point. My loss came when I looked at each of them on that special day and realized they weren't babies anymore. That a rite of passage had occurred while I was making peanut butter and jelly sandwiches. My babies were gone, and in their places were a very mature little boy and girl. I didn't let myself feel that loss until they were safely in school and I was on my way home. Then I cried.

Try some of these on for size—what's the ending?

- Wedding
- Graduation from high school or college
- First job
- Divorce
- Birth of a child
- First day at work
- Nursing home
- Misplacing a valued object
- Missing a phone call

Some of these are clearer than others, aren't they? But with each a loss is there, even if the beginning holds all the joy and happiness we wish for.

Our ending as Self-Sufficients definitely requires time to grieve. Once the light of day shines on our extremism and we begin to see it clearly, we can step back and look at the person who made those decisions in a more empathetic way. "I must have been so afraid." "I couldn't take one more rejection." "I wanted life to be so controlled." As we make the commitment to adjust the behavior that resulted, we feel protective for the self that had to respond in such a fearful way. We need to grieve for that approach to life. We'll need to learn to let go of that extreme aspect of ourselves.

The first time I heard the expression *work through*, I wasn't sure what that meant. Just being conscious of what we're feeling, getting in touch with the emotion, is part of the work. Then, through journaling, exercise, talking with others, or working with a counselor, we can work through that emotion and move on. There is no time frame, no expectation that on a certain date at a certain time, you will be finished and able to check it off and move on. It's a process, a difficult one. Through the grief process you'll have an opportunity—the opportunity to learn more about yourself.

What Will We Experience in Our Ending?
In preparation, let's think about the emotions and thoughts we might experience when we decide to change our behavior from being a Self-Sufficient. We:

- won't have all the control or perceive that we do
- might feel angry that we need to make changes

We'll:

- set ourselves up for rejection
- feel like we're bothering other people
- have to react to others in a different way
- go against what we have been taught all our lives

- experience many stress symptoms
- constantly have to do a sales job on the new behavior
- need to work to stop certain behaviors, like only taking care of others
- have to look at ourselves
- have to figure out what our needs are
- feel unsafe
- feel more vulnerable—a state we've fought to avoid

It's a big decision we're making. No wonder we need preparation. No wonder life has to be awful for us to reach out for something new. And where is this middle, this balance everyone talks about? We know extremism (it has a clear boundary), but we don't know anything about this never-never land everyone calls balance, and it makes us feel stressed just to talk about going there. Thank goodness persistence is one of our virtues. We're banking on all this work taking us to somewhere better, less stressful.

The Neutral Zone

Dr. Bridges also says that humans can't stop and start something simultaneously. I'm reminded of a Dallas corporation that had gone through a large downsizing. Over four hundred friends, colleagues, and team members had lost their jobs. So, when the company planned a large picnic three days hence to roll out the new mission statement and get all the remaining employees on board, the workers boycotted the picnic. They couldn't move from an ending to a beginning that quickly.

We need a neutral zone between our endings and beginnings in order to make the change. Perhaps if we had factored a neutral zone into our diets and exercise programs we would have been more successful.

The neutral zone, according to Dr. Bridges, contains three important elements:

1. Healing
2. Risk taking
3. Looking for opportunity

Part of the healing process that we start in the ending continues in the neutral zone. For some it will extend beyond the new beginning. I'm reminded of a client who called after she'd been in a new position about two months. "I awoke this morning, having finally accepted that life 'dealt me that card' and committed to this new position in a whole new way."

The Stress of the Neutral Zone
Working in the Dallas market meant many outplaced individuals coming from oil companies. Some of them were leaders in the field, vast accomplishments under their belts. One in particular stands out. Recognized as one of the pioneers in oil field methods, he was lost when lack of domestic exploration downsized his huge company. Sitting in my office, he couldn't keep the tears at bay; he said it was the first time he had cried since he was a boy, and he felt ashamed that he'd let his emotions break through.

Over the next months, I watched the struggle as he tried to reinvent himself. How do you sell yourself when you aren't sold? What finally broke the spell was his wife and three teenaged kids. Dad had been away most of their childhoods. Now Dad was here and available. He started coaching a soccer team; he could step into the breach for his wife in the endless carpooling.

As his life started to come into balance, he became someone else, someone he'd lost along the way. He still had a strong work ethic. He wanted to continue to be productive, but he also began to see that he had cheated himself of his children's early years and a stronger relationship with his wife. The outcome was a pizza franchise in a small Texas community that would allow him the balance the crisis had created.

When participants in workshops balk at a neutral zone, I try to give them another way to think about it. Think of a car in neutral. The power is on. You just haven't decided in which direction you're going.

There will be stress, plenty of it, but who knows more about stress than we do? If there is a better life for us, a chance to realize who we were really meant to be, then what's a little extra stress if it's an investment with returns: less stress, more life enjoyment, more fulfillment, feeling part of something greater than ourselves, having to take less responsibility for others and being able to focus more on where we want to go.

The Nine Steps for Successful Stress Management

1. Learn how to balance with refocusing. Gardening? Crafting? Playing with children? Praying? Going to the movies? Hiking? Tennis? Golf? Reading a good book? Researching on the Internet? All of these have a fun element, but they also have a stress-relieving element to them. They get us away from the stress causer for a little while. They refocus us.

However, beware! We Self-Sufficients tend to be extremist in everything we do—so if we're going to garden, the Martha Stewart standard takes over and we find ourselves in the Best Camellia contest. We'll have to guard against being pulled off our original goal. Remember we're just refocusing, not starting a new career.

2. *Design an exercise program.* Exercising is one of the best strategies for a stress management program. "Keep moving!" It doesn't matter what we do—walking, jogging, swimming, bicycling—it all gets the endorphins pumping and gives us a better perspective on life in general.

3. *Learn a relaxation technique.* Relaxation techniques have proven to be consistently effective with clients I've counseled. When I'm doing workshops and we practice this technique, participants give it the highest marks. It takes discipline and commitment, but it's worth it.

Like everything else, this has a preparation too. Make sure you can't hear the phone and that no one will interrupt you. Find a place where you're comfortable (a comfortable chair, for example). Close your eyes and become aware of the feeling of the chair beneath you. Now, slowly start to concentrate on your breathing. After a few minutes, when you have become much more relaxed, start at your feet. Feel the floor beneath them. Feel them grow heavier as you relax them, letting all the muscles go. Slowly move up to your ankles, calves, and thighs, letting them grow heavier, allowing them to relax. After a period of time, move to your stomach and buttocks. Go through the same relaxation process, giving time to allow relaxation to flow into each area. After a time, go back to concentrating on your breathing, experiencing relaxation with each breath. Now relax your chest and back, arms and fingers, neck and head, including your eyes, nose, mouth, chin, and cheeks. Feel the relaxation as you return to concentrating on your breathing.

After practicing for a while, you will notice your breathing becoming very shallow, giving your body a time to rest, recoup. You'll feel a total sense of peace and quiet within yourself. You will begin to feel at one with yourself and the world around you.

When I took a course in relaxation in the early eighties, my teachers suggested that we "practice" twice a day for about twenty minutes each time. I knew that was unrealistic for me. With two children, elderly parents, and a full-time job, I had to get up thirty minutes earlier just to work one session in. Even so, I could almost immediately tell a difference in my energy and outlook.

Did this keep me from having panic attacks? No. But after I began these exercises, I was a happier person.

There's something about giving yourself a gift that reminds you that you deserve to be relaxed, that you deserve for life to be good. I look upon it as a minivacation in my day.

4. Be good to yourself. Speaking of gifts, this should be a time of being downright good to yourself. Anytime we go through significant change, our resistance is down. An extra cup of coffee while watching the sun come up—a walk through a bookstore—a leisurely lunch all by yourself with no errands on the agenda—whatever it is that makes you feel special and rewarded will buoy your resistence.

I love to go to bookstores to just forget about everything. Where do you go for that kind of payoff? Don't walk—run! Build it into your day like a doctor's appointment or a meeting.

It's absolutely amazing what happens. After a while, you notice your self-esteem is rising. If you're important enough for a gift each day in the middle of your hectic, squirrel-cage life, then you must be very important indeed. Give it a try—it works!

5. Get more sleep—quality sleep. Sleep deprivation is epidemic in this country. Late at night, while you should be sleeping, may be when you find the time to figure out the software from work, clean the house, or do the million other things daylight hours don't allow. Aren't we Self-Sufficients 24/7? Doesn't it feed our achievement-based self-esteem to believe we can work around the clock?

But we need sleep to be more productive and energized. And sleep does not mean the catnap you take when you finally get to bed before you have to go again. It means eight hours of sleep that feel rejuvenating and healing. Our sleep habits have gotten out of balance with the rest of us, and we need a strong foundation of balance to build our new behavior on.

What will you have to give up to make the adjustments? What won't get done? Feeling human again can be a brand-new experience for some of us who have been pushing ourselves beyond human endurance because we're doing it all.

6. Adopt good eating habits. Yes, we can't even begin to discuss a stress management plan without discussing our eating habits. I'm a chocoholic. What's your thing? If it's stressful to change, then part of our readiness program is supplying ourselves with the nourishment that good food can bring.

Which vitamins fortify us against the effects of stress the most? B vitamins, found especially in grains, veggies, and proteins. What robs these B vitamins from our systems faster than anything other than stress? You guessed it. All those wonderful items we automatically reach for when we're most stressed out: sugar and caffeine. Talk about a vicious cycle. Everywhere we look today, there is information about nutrition. Investigate it. And eat better.

7. Get in touch with nature. Treat yourself to a moment to look at the nature around you. Maybe it'll mean getting in your car and driving to get there. Or just listen to the birds outside of your city window. It's worth the investment. That's another gift you can give yourself.

Recently, I made a long distance move cross-country. The mountains were calling to me. When close friends moved from Dallas to western North Carolina, I went to visit—four times in four years—

before I made the gigantic decision to literally uproot from a city where I had spent 37 years—and go to the mountains. Now on days when things aren't going well, I jump in my car and drive to the top of the mountain. As I look out over the gorgeous expanse, able to see South Carolina, Georgia, Cold Mountain, apple orchards, I begin to quiet myself inside, becoming part of it all and being grateful to just stand there and enjoy. At the same time, I find myself realizing how much a part of the natural rhythm of nature we are and how we fight it by burning the candle at both ends to get everything done. I think of the line from one of Wordsworth's poems, "Nature never did betray the heart that loved her."

8. Put a support team together. I can't even imagine doing this without a group of supporters cheering, "You can do this!" through each bumpy spot on the road to no longer being severely self-sufficient. Having others who are experiencing the same need to change will feel like a lifeline at times.

Which brings up the concern about being vulnerable again. When you share with others that something isn't working, you are sharing your most vulnerable self.

So putting a support system in place will take time, patience with yourself, and all the determination you can muster. One trusted person at a time. How about other Self-Sufficients you hang around with? Maybe their lives are on burnout too. Ask them to join you.

That wall is strong and it will resist, but the symptoms or discontent will only grow worse. How will you prepare yourself to just begin? Will you be willing?

9. Take inventory of the strengths you bring. What strengths that you've developed from being Self-Sufficient will you be able to bring to this?

- Persistence—bull-dog persistence! If you put into play the persistence with which you've tackled tasks over the years into finding the middle, who knows what can happen?
- Determination! We are the most determined of the species. Once our radar is set on something, we will get there, no matter what. Where has your determination gotten you? How can you direct it to become more balanced?
- We're self-motivated, par excellence! No one has to lay out a schedule for us. We're expert at prioritizing and getting things done. So how will you apply this skill to modifying your way to less extreme self-sufficiency?

Risking

Dr. Bridges tells us that we have time to risk in the neutral zone, to experiment and find out what works and what doesn't. The risk in changing or modifying our self-sufficient behavior will be letting others see us in a more vulnerable light.

Reaching that pivot point where we can no longer maintain the status quo takes courage and risk. We'll be in uncharted waters; we'll need our support group. There will be days when we want to turn back—back to that hot water that was our comfort zone.

Can you risk admitting just one area where you need help? Ask just one person if he or she can help you? Maintain your composure while the fear feels like it's overcoming you? Open the wall just a crack to let others in? Be surprised when the world doesn't end?

Opportunity

There are lots of opportunities in the neutral zone:

- Looking at life differently through others' eyes and experiences
- Exploring and not knowing what you will find

- Saying you don't know something and letting it go at that
- Saying "No, I can't," without explaining why for ten minutes
- Going in search of the mediocre, and all that means
- Feeling comfortable when not in the one-up position
- Recognizing your strengths to give you courage to acknowledge your weak areas
- Acknowledging each step to being open as if it were the night of the Academy Awards®
- Celebrating the failures more than the successes—they get you closer to the "real you"
- Slowing down—what seems like warp speed to others is a snail's pace for you
- Just for one day at a time, not expecting a huge output from yourself, not beating yourself up when you actually enjoy a day
- Seeing that you can live through each of these small advances, that you actually feel better about yourself— as if there's an adventure that you're just learning about

The New Beginning— From Self-Sufficient to Sufficient-Self

If Self-Sufficiency Syndrome is the problem, what am I calling the solution? Isn't that your new beginning? You're right! Like a caterpillar—slowly, gradually, as you work through the solutions I'll present, you take on the characteristics of a butterfly. I call that the *Sufficient-Self!*

No longer closed off and giving in to the fear, you become more open to change. More open to many things. Let's do a point-by-point comparison as shown in Figure 5.1:

Self-Sufficient to Sufficient-Self	
Self-Sufficient	**Sufficient-Self**
Feel sense of isolation	Feel sense of belonging
Driven	Persevering
Controlling	Cooperative
Prefer competing against others	Open to collaborating with others
Demand perfection	Accept imperfections
Rigid	Flexible
Reluctant to ask for help	Willing to ask for help
Afraid to fail	Learn from mistakes
Assume total responsibility	Share responsibility/delegate
Don't deserve help	Entitled to receive help
Must be the giver	Balance giving and taking
Secretly feel insecure	Adequate and confident
Feel alone and separate	Feel connected and supported

Figure 5.1: Self-Sufficient to Sufficient-Self

Recognize any of this? This was your Circling Exercise in Chapter Four. You may want to check and see how many you selected. Now let's translate this list into day-to-day living. What if . . .

- you awoke one morning rested and excited about the day ahead

- you looked in the mirror and really understood the value of the person looking back at you
- you felt valued by others and could ask for help because you realized that it was more productive and fulfilling
- as a result of this, you understood that you were part of something greater than yourself and that isolation was not the answer
- on any given day, you could balance your independence with depending on others that you could trust
- if you made a mistake, you were able to learn from it
- you began to define yourself differently
- through all these things, you realized that the give and take resulted in your feeling accepted as if you belonged

Sound like it's too good to be true? Nope! It's the promise I offer Self-Sufficients—the ability through hard work to become all these things. In the following chapters, I'll show you how. Instead of relying only on ourselves (Self-Sufficient) we reverse the process and rely on our being "enough" to reach out to others (Sufficient-Self). What a beginning!

This new beginning is yours alone, to be customized and decorated as you wish. It has boundaries, but only small pieces of a wall may remain. It is the best possible you—balanced between accomplishment and relationships. These changes can happen. But being ready—giving yourself a chance to look at the barriers and the pitfalls and be prepared for them—will ensure your success. Mentally, emotionally, physically, and spiritually, you can't say you are truly willing until you have:

- thought carefully through your actions and their repercussions

- enlisted others to be on your "support for change" team
- begun to grieve the losses
- put your conscious stress management plan into action
- developed a plan for change in your neutral zone
- identified your strengths
- visualized your new beginning
- taken that first step

Now . . . let's begin!

PART II

Get Your Balance: Become Interdependent

CHAPTER SIX

Interdependence: Moving Toward the Middle

Interdependence is and ought to be as much
the ideal of man as self-sufficiency.
Man is a social being.
MAHATMA GANDHI

We tend to think in a straight line, don't we? You know—beginning, middle, end; departure, flight, arrival; morning, noon, night. Everything in a straight time-line sequence.

Let me invite you to try another type of thinking that applies to becoming less severely self-sufficient. Think of a pendulum swinging from side to side until slowing to a settling point in the center of the two extremes. A place of balance. A place where we're not trying to do it all ourselves, nor are we relying on others to do it for us.

In this situation, the destination point is not at either end but in the middle. We're suggesting that we develop from dependence to independence until finally we find ourselves centered in interdependence as illustrated in Figure 6.1.

In the context of exploring the Self-Sufficient style of giving but not receiving, I'd like you to consider the concept of personal interdependence.

When you reach the interdependent stage of personal developmental growth, you demonstrate the ability to:

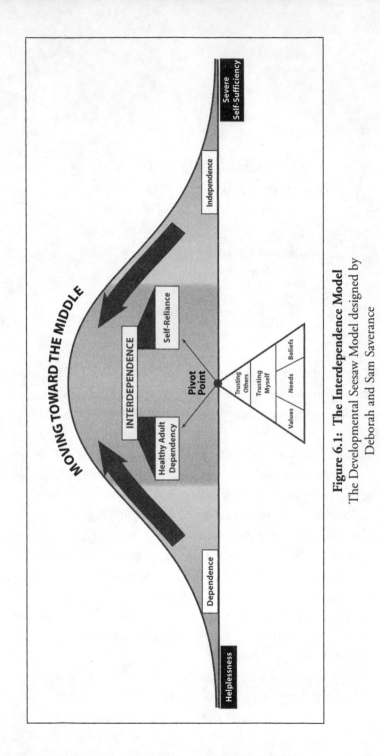

Figure 6.1: The Interdependence Model
The Developmental Seesaw Model designed by
Deborah and Sam Saverance

- ask and receive help when you want it
- rely on yourself to act alone when you need to
- understand the benefits and sense of fulfillment from interacting
- feel equally okay about choosing either direction

Personal interdependence is a sum, a mixture, an interaction of your abilities to appropriately depend on others or to choose to rely on yourself in any given situation.

It's the ability to maintain a flexible position balanced in the center of the seesaw, prepared to pivot with grace and confidence toward either self-reliance on one side or toward a quality we'll call *healthy adult dependency* at the other.

Once again, though, simple doesn't always mean easy. Just like all the other worthwhile goals you've met, moving toward the middle takes effort. But unlike all the other goals you've met, the unique reward this time will be that as you move away from the behaviors of Self-Sufficiency Syndrome, you won't be alone . . . you'll have people in your life with whom you'll be interdependent!

The Collaborative Spirit of Interdependence

I like the way psychologist Kathryn D. Cramer explains why it takes effort for any of us, much less the Self-Sufficient, to adopt an interdependent perspective:

> We have been shaped into independent learners and performers, ready at any moment to defend our position, debate to win, and take the credit for our own ideas or actions. We have been led to believe that we are ultimately operating alone, and therefore we strive as individuals, contribute as individuals, and judge ourselves to be more or

less successful on an individual basis. Like the law students who steal books from their college library so no one else can read them, we fear the competence of others who might outshine us. . . . Overreliance on an independent mind-set prevents us personally and collectively from reaping the rewards of creative collaboration.

The writing of this book is an example of both the personal and collaborative types of interdependence we're talking about. When Deborah and I met several years ago, I was already hot on this topic in my head. As we got to know each other and I mentioned some of my thoughts, we recognized that we both showed signs and symptoms of Self-Sufficiency Syndrome and the problems that go with it. We laughed about the lengths we would go to take care of everything and everybody in our lives, expecting ourselves to do it all, all by ourselves. The more we saw we had in common, the more willing we were to risk being open about the downside of being so accomplishment-driven.

A funny thing happened—instead of losing face with each other as we admitted to not being as *completely* together as everyone thought, we gained a growing sense of mutual trust, understanding, and relief about peeking out from behind the "I'm fine—I can handle it" wall of self-sufficiency. Can you believe it?—We actually started asking each other for help! To be a sounding board for the other's doubts and concerns or to give perspective on an issue to which one or the other of us was too close to be objective. Confiding to another person that yes, we could, possibly, perhaps now and then, use a bit of a helping hand was a major breakthrough.

The time came when it was obvious to me that a book needed to be written—so we spent many hours over lunch or coffee while I brainstormed and bantered around ideas and concepts.

I am happy to report that by that time I had moved toward the middle enough to realize that I needed help on this project—I admitted to myself that although I could write it alone, it would not turn out to be what I envisioned if I did. You see, my communication strength is speaking, not writing. Lest you think one's the same as the other, let me assure you they are not. I decided to approach the one person who knew more about my thoughts on self-sufficiency than anyone else, my friend Deborah. Did I mention that her field is communication disorders, and that she much prefers writing over speaking? What do you do with a speaker who'd rather not write, and a writer who'd rather not speak? You put them together and get a book about collaboration by two people who are collaborating!

Through all of this—the self-disclosure, the brainstorming, the late-night phone debates, the cross-country e-mailing of ideas, concepts and drafts, the mutual sweating of deadlines, the need to depend on the other where one lacked ability, we learned that we are our most fulfilled when we have the opportunity to interact from a balanced position of demonstrating both a healthy dependency and a solid sense of self-reliance.

Translation: interdependence makes us happier. Even so, for two Self-Sufficients all this disruption of our well-constructed status quo has been challenging and, at times, humbling. It's graduation from where we've been and kindergarten to where we're going. But with all the moving I've done in my life, packing up and making the trek out of the lonely sierra of extreme self-sufficiency toward the middle ground of interdependence is by far the best and most life-changing move I've made.

What We Learned

Interdependent people carry forward a strong component of self-reliance developed during their independent stage. They know from experience that they can rely on themselves to make good choices, reach their goals and get a job done. But in contrast to the Self-Sufficient, this is not their preferred modus operandi. They have learned the benefits of actively communicating and collaborating with others that they've grown to know, respect, and trust. Interdependent people understand that this kind of collaboration with trustworthy friends, colleagues and family members has the potential for richer results both in a practical and in a spiritual sense.

Practically speaking, they know that more can be accomplished, more effectively, more creatively, and with a greater return, when tapping the resources of the many. And they've learned that, with the right people, this can actually feel good— the interaction, the flow, the shared sweat, the access to a larger pool of talent, the mutual investment of thought and focus, and the possibility for greater-than-expected results.

Perhaps the most enriching reward of living interdependently is the deeper, more spiritual bond we enjoy with others, regardless of the outcome of the project or task at hand. As we bring the best that we are to the table of interdependence, we become eligible to experience a deeper level of fulfillment that surpasses our basic needs. We begin to sense our common ground, our common connection with others and that we are an integral part of something vastly important, something bigger than ourselves. We perceive ourselves as valuable, and we feel that we belong. "In your authentic exchanges with the people you value, a sense of community is born." says Cramer, "And any time a community is bound together by an inspiring vision, the invisible interests that connect people to each other are realized more fully and creatively." When we become familiar with the strength of connectedness that comes with living interdependently, the light dawns, and we see that participation itself is its own reward. We will have morphed into becoming a *Sufficient-Self!*

Interdependence Comes As
Standard Equipment on All Models

The idea that each of us is not only a *me*, but a part of a *we*, is not new. Philosophers, educators, psychologists, and social scientists have observed, studied, and long written about the human individual as being a part of something greater than himself—that along with a sense of self as separate and unique, we require a sense of sameness and wholeness, of sharing the human condition with others. It seems that this is fundamental to our species—the need to bring our piece to a bigger puzzle, the innate desire to feel a part of a "we-ness."

——— —

If all this "natural" stuff feels unnatural to you, it may be because you've had to separate from the *we* aspect of your nature just to survive. You found that keeping yourself to yourself seemed to work better in your set of circumstances—or maybe you were taught that complete self-sufficiency was the appropriate, mature way to live. Either way, you see the dilemma: when you're stuck in a place where you're barricaded off from interdepending with others, you are cut off from enjoying the full expression of who you are.

Tough Q&A

Q: Look, I've gotten by with living self-sufficiently for a long time—will moving toward interdependence at this point really improve my life?

A: Fact is, sooner or later, we all have to depend on others—our bodies can handle only so many tune-ups and replacement parts.

Research shows that individuals at every age appear to function better and be more resilient when they experience others standing behind them with love and affection. So the answer would be, "yes"—even baby steps toward a more interdependent perspective in your relationships will improve your life.

Q: I've learned to network with people professionally and socially—isn't that the same as becoming personally and collaboratively interdependent?

A: Most networking relationships are built on the premise, "I'll support your goals if you'll support mine." It's what psychologists Margaret Clark and Judson Mills studied and called an *exchange relationship*—where one gets back for giving some benefit to the other, a quid pro quo, a relationship governed by equity concerns. The type of interdependent relationships we're describing would line up with what the researchers call a *communal relationship*—one that's governed by a responsiveness to the other's needs, where we feel no exploitation or need to track the equity of who is contributing what—the focus is on how one's actions can contribute to meeting needs. When balanced in a state of interdependence, we say, "I'll support your goals, and in so doing, I'm supporting a vision of building community—something larger than ourselves." We are free to "pay it forward," knowing that there are those we can depend upon if and when we need support.

Q: Are you saying that to continue to develop, I need to give up my hard-earned independence? Honestly, if I start depending on others again, won't that be a step backwards?

A: Not if you bring the wisdom, discretion, and healthy self-reliance you've gained from your independent stage with you. A.W. Chickering, noted educator and psychologist, argued that, "in its highest form, the development of autonomy does not simply involve the development of freedom to choose freely and act independent of outside influences, but also involves the development of freedom that recognizes one's dependence and obligations to others."

Learning to depend on others in the right way and the right time is a defining characteristic of moving into a mature state of interdependence. As Robert F. Bornstein and Mary A. Languirand so aptly describe in their book, *Healthy Dependency: Leaning on Others Without Losing Yourself*, it is a state of personal strength and confidence. For those of us who didn't get a solid foundation in this kind of dependency as kids, there is hope. Not by going backwards and rummaging in the past, but by looking forward to providing for ourselves a healthy mature alternative when the situation calls for something other than self-reliance.

Healthy Adult Dependency

To bring us back toward the higher middle ground of interdependence from our extreme position of severe self-sufficiency, we'll have to add some qualities from the opposite side of the continuum—dependency. Only this time, it's not that childhood dependency some of us hated. It's an adult dependency we arrive at through a relearning process. Using all those skills and strengths we've amassed as Self-Sufficients, we're able to make this a healthy dependency, a healthy adult dependency. Look at some of the differences shown in Figure 6.2.

Being able to access healthy adult dependency is the most critical factor in successfully treating Self-Sufficiency Syndrome. For the Self-Sufficient it is the quality we're missing under the umbrella of Interdependence. Look at the model on Interdependence shown previously in Figure 6.1. Interdependence is only achieved by bringing all the best from our healthy adult dependency and our more

HAD	ECD
Personal choice	No personal choice
Individual control	Others in control
Feeling of connection	Feeling of helplessness
Competent to depend on self or others	Must depend on others
Built on sense of self-trust and resiliency	Based on fear of abandonment, neglect, and so forth

**Figure 6.2: Healthy Adult Dependency (HAD) vs.
Early Childhood Dependency (ECD)**

tempered self-reliance. It will take the most courage to acquire and has the potential of bringing you the greatest rewards. I've accomplished my goal if you only remember the positive possibilities of practicing healthy adult dependency alongside self-reliance. In a nutshell, we become our most healthy selves when we acknowledge, accept, and joyfully live out of a balanced sense of needing others and others needing us. It's indeed the balance!

All remaining chapters of this book are about how you can make this quality a part of your life. Looking ahead, I'll show you how to:

• Explore and get to know yourself better. Without a strong sense of who you are, what you value and believe, your dependence could fall back to feeling like childhood dependence when you have to count on others to give you what you couldn't provide yourself. Erikson says a mature identity involves both *individuation* and *connectedness*. That means that the give and take we enjoy in our relationships with others reflects back to us information that helps form our self-identity.

- Examine and reconstruct your attitude and beliefs. We've taken independence to such an extreme. If we can undo some of the beliefs that got us there, maybe we'll become more flexible to taking risks and depending on someone else.
- Be brutally honest with yourself about your values and whether your actions reflect what you say is most important in your life. About how important your relationships really are in your life. And then alter your expectations of yourself, others, and life in general to match your values.
- Face your fear of failing. You will need to accept how instructive failure can be and take advantage of those lessons.
- Strengthen your ability to trust. You'll need to be willing to learn about trusting in areas of life that you have typically shut off from others and kept to yourself. Healthy adult dependency will require a willingness to be vulnerable.

Does this sound like an impossible task? Well, don't worry, I'll take it one step at a time, because I truly understand that every small step in the direction of interdependence is a huge leap of faith for the Self-Sufficient. Keeping your eyes on the prize will help to motivate you. Learning healthy adult dependency sets you up for some pretty significant rewards.

The Potential Payoffs of Interdependence

1. Payoff: Freedom from Fear

Did all my fear of giving up control and letting others help go away? No! I'm convinced that some of my very early fears have melded into my being and that the acceptance, empathy, and understanding of those fears is the way I will be able to best live the rest of my life.

I still have work to do, but the fear that I was all there was—that it was all up to me—that nothing would be done well or complete—that no one would be able to live their lives without my advice and direction is gone.

I'll admit, at first it felt very selfish to me. I had never allowed myself such self-serving thoughts. But then I was able to see that this was the balance I had missed before, that I was part of the equation, that I had a birthright along with everyone else, that I too deserved the attention and support to live my life out fully—and that, my friends, was immensely freeing.

2. Payoff: Freedom to Live and Let Live

When I made the choice to "live and let live," accepting that I didn't know what was best for others, that most of the time I did not even know what was best for me, it was as though the shackles came off.

A great burden that I had carried all my life fell away. I was able to breathe life in for the very first time. Oh, I had a long way to go, but it was a moment like no other I have ever had.

3. Payoff: Permission to Give and Take in Full Circle

I'll bet you've heard the expression, "the teacher teaches what the teacher needs to learn." Nothing could be truer for me. In networking workshops over the years, I had always espoused the networking axiom, "Feed and take care of your network and your network will feed and take care of you." That when I helped others, I was in a sense transmitting positive energy out into the world, and that if my "receiver" was functioning, much like a radio or TV, the signals would eventually return to me in a complete circle. It was quite an awakening to realize that I had been blocking the reception of these signals with "my wall." The blessing of receiving was interrupted—it just couldn't penetrate all that fear.

Realizing that receiving can be a gift—that was huge for me! My friend Jo Ellen had said the same thing to me some forty years before, but I'm a slow learner, "when will you give me the dignity of helping you?"

4. *Payoff: A Lighter Load*

The stress of doing it all, all by myself decreased significantly, when I was able to trust and accept the help of so many willing participants in my life. The pressure associated with my perpetual to-do list diminished because more of it was getting done—many hands do indeed make light work. As I stepped back from assuming total responsibility for everything and everyone in my life and humbly allowed myself to lean on others occasionally, I experienced a sense of huge relief on all levels—mentally, physically, emotionally, and spiritually.

5. *Payoff: Depth in My Close Relationships*

After the shift in my self-sufficient mind-set toward interdependence, I admitted that I longed for a deeper connection to the wonderful people in my life and that I would have to come out from behind my defensive wall to have that. I would have to be more balanced in my presentation of myself, which of course meant I would have to be willing to reveal a real person—warts and all. It wasn't enough for me to define myself as one able to listen to the struggles of others, I had to ante up and admit to having struggles myself. On this level, reciprocity, a word I had bandied about in my networking workshops, took on a new meaning: belonging in exchange for vulnerability. It is only when I took the leap and opened up to those I decided to trust, that I felt for the first time that I truly belonged—belonged in a community and belonged to myself, claiming my right to a place in the world.

6. *Payoff: The Beauty of Balance*

Life out in the far reaches of self-sufficiency was frenetic. But I realized that being busy is not the same as being fulfilled. That sometimes moving forward means standing still—listening, being aware of all that is, not just what I must make happen next. That a life too busy to appreciate the bliss of breathing is a life wasting precious gifts that all the work in the world can't provide. If I didn't have enough balance in my life to drink in the color of the leaves, or even notice the sunset—well, then, for me those things might as well not even exist. In the quest of striving for more, I was wasting what was already mine. In one grand leap of faith, I stepped off the treadmill and started strolling side by side with others, taking time to feel the sunshine and smell those roses that were there all the time. I have found the beauty of life from this new place of balance to be breathtaking.

CHAPTER SEVEN

Fortify Your Fulcrum:
Internal Support

*In oneself lies the whole world and if you know how
to look and learn, then the door is there
and the key is in your hand.*

J. KRISHNAMURTI

How do you reach a place of balance that allows you to enjoy a more interdependent life? Well, if we go back and consider the way a seesaw works, we get some valuable clues from the physics. If you want to balance a seesaw, the center structure known as the fulcrum must be solid, able to support weight, and provide stability and flexibility. The same goes for you. If you want a balanced life, your center structure needs to be solid and complete, allowing you to move in from the self-sufficient edge toward the interdependent middle. Why is this balancing act so hard for Self-Sufficients?

A few weeks ago, I was visiting with a new physician's assistant in my doctor's office. "What do you speak on?" she asked, glancing down at my file and noting that I was a professional speaker.

Seeing this as a wonderful opportunity to do a little informal polling, I replied, "Actually, I'm in the middle of writing a book about people who can't ask for help. It's about the Self-Sufficiency Syndrome."

Her hand shot up so fast it startled me. "That's me," she volunteered.

"Why do you think?" I queried.

"Oh, that's easy. I don't trust people." And out the door she shot, leaving me to ponder.

Trust: Lost and Found

If you're like I am, then you have always struggled with trust. Now, I could dig around and tell you all the gory reasons why, but I'm not sure at this point it would help us with our project. Suffice it to say, what I finally discovered is that my inability to trust at two different levels represented fundamental missing pieces in my developmental puzzle—probably the most critical pieces to reconstruct in treating Self-Sufficiency Syndrome.

Level One: Trusting Others

We can't trust that others will be there for us, so we do everything all by ourselves. We take old experiences and transpose them on every new situation, clinging to the mantra, "I can't afford to trust anyone but myself." Because we believe this so deeply, we may fulfill our own prophecy by attracting the very people who will substantiate that we're right about this.

But let's speculate how your life might change if you woke up tomorrow with the intention to extend trust to others. You would:

- be able to delegate to those you could trust to do a good job
- start to balance your drive to achieve with putting more effort into forming trustful relationships

- move to release bits and pieces of your burden of responsibilities, thus decreasing the intensity of your daily stress
- open the way to experience the diverse benefits of collaboration and, with the increase in productivity and creativity, confirm the old adage, "Two heads (or three, four, or five) are better than one."

Is it realistic that you will be able to just wake up and change all your ingrained behaviors? Of course not. Changed behavior is a result of changed thinking, and for you to step back from doing it all, you'll need to work on that important shift. Hopefully the work we've done thus far has brought you to this important place. Can it happen overnight? Nope. It will take the commitment you've already shown and all the strengths we've referenced before. But, I assure you, it will be well worth the work.

Here's a list of some of the major shifts in thinking you'll need to make. How many of these items have you already convinced yourself to make?

1. Depending on someone else does not mean that you are not able and strong.
2. Adjusting your performance expectations on a case-by-case basis can have more valuable results in building relationships than pushing for perfection each and every time.
3. Taking risks is the key to growth. That's as true for risking and failing as it is for risking and succeeding.
4. Trusting your intuition. Some of us Self-Sufficients grew up not trusting our own intuition and instincts. The truth is that most of us have keener instincts than others.

If you will start by working on these thoughts, you will be taking the first step in changing how you act. I'll provide you with more suggestions and support regarding how to further tweak your behavior in Chapter Eight.

Trust is the bridge to balanced giving and receiving. It allows us to open our hearts and minds to others. It allows us to take measured risks. Granted, we could get burned. And we would be crazy not to be concerned about this. But, that's when reconstructing the second level of missing trust becomes essential to building that inner strength, that solid fulcrum that allows us to find riches in rubble.

Level Two: Trusting Ourselves

A telltale sign that we are making the shift from being a Self-Sufficient to a Sufficient-Self is when we can trust others with the calm assurance that our strong fulcrum will anchor and steady us if we are disappointed. We learn that it's only by taking prudent risks and making occasional mistakes in extending trust to others that we enable our own development. Sure, it stings when someone lets us down, but with a strong core sense of who we are and what we're worth, we can survive these moments and live to see another day—becoming wiser about choosing the people whom we will trust and learning more about ourselves in the process.

Like me, you may have always prided yourself in being strong enough not to need too much introspection or self-analysis. The word *strong* can have several connotations. You may pride yourself on being emotionally strong.

A client told me recently that growing up she had been told to be "strong" for her ailing mother. She sat in front of me, at age sixty, still being strong for mother, long gone. I understand that. Although you may be able to lift 50 pounds and never break a sweat, or respond stoically to stuff that makes others crash and burn, how do you feel in those quiet honest moments that you allow yourself? Do you have a calm solid assurance that no matter what happens, you're going to be okay? If you woke up one day unable to prove yourself through performance, would you still have a sufficient sense of who you are?

In 1987, in the midst of my panic attacks, one of the very first thoughts I had was that I couldn't even trust myself anymore. I felt at that point that even my body had let me down, forcing me to face the fact that staying in control was something I could not control, that my master solution did not have a lifetime guarantee. Suddenly all the security I had built on my own solid self-sufficiency crumbled. I realized that the trust I thought I had in myself was based exclusively on what I could do, not on the value of who I was—and to tell you the truth, I didn't really know there was a difference! Finally unable to keep up my frenzied pace, I became unsure of who I was. A light came on when it occurred to me that you can't trust someone you don't know.

One level of trust is built on another. Not only do we need to trust ourselves first before we can trust others, we also need to know who it is that we are learning to trust. That means slowing down and taking a sincere internal inventory. And I'm not talking about a résumé of what you can do. I mean coming to know at a deeper level what you *truly* value, what you *really* need, and what you *fundamentally* believe.

Without the knowledge of these three components, your true identity can remain hidden, even to yourself. With this knowledge, you gain the understanding of who you really are at your core. Identifying, acknowledging, and accepting this essential information about yourself and then honoring this knowledge by acting congruently is the key to building a healthy trust in yourself.

Operation Introspection

The goal is to fortify your fulcrum. The objectives to reach this goal are to (1) increase your willingness to trust others by (2) building a healthy self-trust and (3) researching your core values, needs, and beliefs. My strategy to help you meet these objectives is to do an internal inventory that will spotlight how much of your behavior is unsupported by your values, needs, and beliefs. We'll consider how, as your actions become more congruent with these core components, the unique picture of your life puzzle will become more recognizable, more focused, and more complete (see Figure 7.1). That's the payoff.

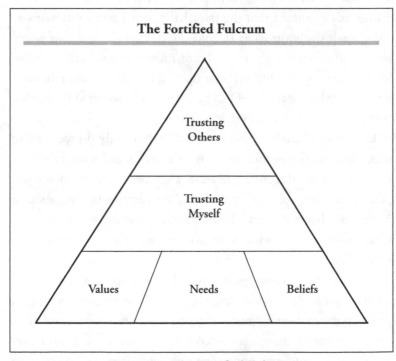

Figure 7.1: The Fortified Fulcrum
Source: Deborah and Sam Saverance

Here's the price tag: you'll need to be very introspective. We Self-Sufficients shy away from this important exercise as long as we can, finding all kinds of diversions to avoid it—focusing on everyone else, staying task-oriented, doing it all, all by ourselves so that we have no time for introspection. Here's the good news I can offer you: although you can't change the past, you can use all the data we gather from such an analysis to construct an alternative to the pieces of trust you missed—a mature alternative that opens the door to interdependence, an alternative I explained earlier, healthy adult dependency. Are you ready, willing, and able to make some important changes?

Core Component #1:
Your Values

What motivates you? What creates a bounce in your step when things are going well and the will to plow forward when things are not? What makes you feel you're on the right track, that your life is purposeful and your energy well spent? Whatever those things are, behold your values! Like a tape measure, if you lay your values down beside your behavior, their congruence—or lack of—should give you a good idea of whether you are being true to who you really are.

Values can fall in various categories. We have relationship values, work values, life values, play values, and so on. A *core value* is one that is so important to you that you wouldn't be who you are without it.

In Figure 7.2, there are some examples that others have mentioned, and there is space for you to jot down more that come to mind.

Core Values		
Education	Love	Self-Respect
Accomplishment	Family	Beauty
Money	Relationships	Courage
Security	Needing to be needed	Wisdom
Career satisfaction	Spirituality/Religion	Self-Sufficiency
Success	Service to others	Honesty
Fame	Community	Self-Development
Fun and leisure	Cultural pursuits	Health

Figure 7.2: Core Values
Source: Deborah and Sam Saverance

Inventory Your Values

At first glance this may seem like an easy task, but for the results to be effective it takes some real thought and consideration. Take some quiet, focused time to clarify what you truly care about. Can you put them in a list and prioritize them in order of their significance to you? Try to come up with your three most important values and note them here:

1. _____

2. _____

3. _____

Now, ask yourself if the people who know you well and observe the way you live would be in agreement with or confused or possibly even shocked by what you've listed as your top values. How do you spend your time and resources? Does your actual behavior support what you say is most valuable to you? Another way to put it is: does the way you live your life send a message that is consistent or in conflict with your values? How much of your attention is focused on your top value? For example, many of us would answer "Family" to this one when the truth is we spend most of our actual hours working rather than with family. Oh, I know we rationalize this one, but are we pursuing accomplishments at work when we really could be spending time with family?

These are not easy questions, *especially* for Self-Sufficients. We may have compromised our values so much they are hard to identify. For example, because we tend to be highly competitive, we are able to ignore or set aside our own true values for the sake of winning, reaching the goal, and being the best. Or perhaps when we tried to work on relationships in the past, we've adopted or accommodated the values of others at the expense of our own just to keep the peace, blend in, or be supportive. Be alert if you recognize these symptoms in your behavior, and as you think about what you value, ask, "Is this really *my* value or one that I've inherited, adopted, or assumed for other reasons?"

Now, here is a key question: where did Self-Sufficiency rate on your top three? If you're living a life that is committed to doing it all, all by yourself, aren't you behaving as though it's your most important value? How does that conflict with the value of Family or Relationships? Spirituality? Health? Love? Security? Growth? Self-development? The argument could be made that you are setting up a conflict with every other value when you choose becoming completely self-sufficient as the thing that you value above all else.

Over time, as you seek help and gain skill in resolving these conflicts, you'll feel a growing confidence in your ability to make the decisions that support the way you really want to live.

Action Steps: Ask and Answer

1. Where do you recognize conflicts between your top three
   values and your behavior?

   _____

   _____

   _____

2. If your actions reflected your values, would you be able to
   trust yourself more?

   _____

3. What physical, mental, or emotional symptoms are you
   having as a result of conflict between what you value and
   what you choose to do? Look back at the suggestions in
   Chapter Five for steps you can take to relieve some of your
   stress.

   _____

   _____

   _____

4. What major or minor steps can you take to act consistent with
   your values? Does it involve change in a job? A relationship?

   _____

   _____

5. Who can give you advice and counsel before you act?

_____

_____

6. Go celebrate!

Component #2: Your Needs

I was thinking to myself, "If the world were
just perfect and you didn't have to
ask for anything, if people were
just sensitive to all our needs,
that would be much easier."
JEFF AUBERY, from
The Aladdin Factor

Self-Sufficients are not very comfortable with the idea of having needs unless they are sure *they* can meet them. Remember the story about the woman who got the vase down herself rather than ask her husband for help? Later, when I asked what she needed, this was her answer. "I need to be able to just depend on myself. I don't want anyone to have anything they can throw up to me later." Then there's the woman in a workshop who said if she had to ask someone for something she needed, it wouldn't mean anything to her.

Even if we deny or ignore our needs, we do have needs just like everyone else and deep inside we know it. But, rather than expressing those needs and risking being disappointed, we expect those who really care about us to just know what we need. Mind reading is an unhealthy expectation to put on any relationship, especially if the people you share your life with don't happen to be clairvoyant. You know you really have a significant problem expressing your needs if you'd rather have a fight over someone's inability to read your mind rather than just coming out and asking for what you need.

There is one need that is pretty obvious in the profile of a Self-Sufficient—*we need to be needed*. If pressed to be candid, I think many of us would say it's our greatest need. We've got a lot invested in this one need—so much, in fact, that many of us would have to admit it made our top three values. Because we need to be needed, we surround ourselves with people who need us. This definitely increases our sense of worth, doesn't it? We feel valuable because we're needed, not because we have value without it. When we're feeling low, we just go out and find someone who needs something, and it fixes us right up, making us feel useful, valuable, and, of course, very busy—too busy to look inside and take stock. Don't be surprised when you start identifying your own needs that, due to neglect, you find a wasteland of your own unattended needs.

Inventory Your Needs

All of us need the most basic of things—a roof over our heads, food in our stomachs, clothing to wear. Vast amounts of money are spent each year helping people who are still dependent meet these needs. Self-Sufficients, however, sit on the other end of the seesaw, having long ago made sure that their basic needs are met. It's when you ratchet up the questions about the more abstract but essential needs that they may be slower to answer.

For instance, what emotional needs do you have? Do you need to be respected? Valued? Appreciated? Loved? To feel like you belong? Are these needs being met sufficiently? If not, have you expressed them in a constructive way? Do you know how? If this line of questioning feels uncomfortable to you, join the club. To have to ask to get your needs met sounds "needy." It means you'll have to ask for help, and now you're where you started. The vicious cycle persists.

But, no, not necessarily. As promised early on, suggestions are coming in Chapter Eight regarding how to express your needs and ask for help without giving up your dignity, but for now let's stick with your internal inventory and make sure you know what you really need.

In *The Aladdin Factor,* Jack Canfield and Mark Victor Hansen ask some significant questions to help you figure out what you need:

1. What are you dissatisfied with
   - in your primary relationship?
   - in your relationship with the members of your family?
   - in your relationships at work?
2. Do you want someone to
   - spend more time with you?
   - leave you alone?
   - visit more often?
3. Do you want to
   - feel closer?
   - stop fighting?
   - improve your relationship?
   - feel more comfortable sharing your feelings?

- get something off your chest?
- ask for forgiveness?
- share your dreams?
4. What do you need or want from
   - your spouse?
   - your best friend?
   - your parents?
   - your children?
   - your brothers or sisters?
   - the people you work with?
   - the people you go to school with?
   - your next-door neighbor?
   - your babysitter or housekeeper?
   - the people in your church or synagogue?
   - the people in your support group?

This is quite a comprehensive list that would be extremely valuable to keep in front of us until we start to ask these questions of ourselves automatically. Will we get what we need when we ask for it? Not always. But we'll be able to see the relationship much more clearly than we ever have before. In this trial-and-error learning process, we'll observe relationships where others seem to know how to get anything they need but don't have a clue how to turn around and return the favor. We may also come to understand the actions of friends who have been allowing us "our space" lest they hurt our pride by offering help. We will be surprised at others' surprise at the thought that we ever really needed the things we finally express. This exercise becomes invaluable in really taking a realistic look at some of our relationships with a balanced perspective. But regardless of the results, every time we ask for what we need, we demonstrate that we value ourselves, and this strengthens our self-trust.

I remember vividly the very first time I really asked for what I needed in a business relationship. For years, my key need was the paycheck that helped feed my children. My personal needs were on the bottom rung. As a result, I played the game, didn't rock the boat, and lost respect for myself. As usual, I came at everything from an extremist view because I had no idea where the middle might be. Stay safe, give everything to the job, and don't even think about what you do or don't need. In the meantime, my self-respect suffered horribly!

I was part of a management team and was the only woman. Our direct boss was female, so when we met, if she had any grievances about anyone's work, she would bring it up to me, as though I had done it—then she wouldn't have to confront one of the men.

One day, about four or five months into this job, I had had all I could take. Midway through the list of things I needed to do differently, I found myself standing up and saying, "*I don't need this!* Susan, you and I need to have a personal conversation, but I'll do that tomorrow." Then I walked out.

The next day, before I could schedule an appointment with Susan, she called. Over lunch, she apologized, admitted that she knew she had a problem confronting men, that she was going to get some coaching on it, and that she would never do that again.

My job wasn't lost. What a valuable lesson I have learned about increasing my value to myself. Bringing our giving and receiving into balance in terms of asking for what we need can be vitally important to our sense of well-being and the strength of our fulcrum.

Component # 3: Your Beliefs

This is the most fundamental component of the core you. It would be easy to create a chapter with quotes from past and present sages that could be concisely paraphrased into the statement "You are what you believe." If we can go back and see the events and patterns that formed the beliefs that are driving our current extreme behaviors, we will gain insight about why we're so out of balance. These patterns may originate all the way back to childhood fears. We would never think of wearing a style from thirty years ago, but we're dragging beliefs along that may be even older, and they are still controlling our behavior.

Many of our beliefs from childhood were reactive simply because we were in our dependent stage, when our view of the world was completely influenced by what and who directly shaped our experience. The experiences of our first couple of decades made lasting impressions that forever influence our perspective, regardless of whether we treasure or abhor those that we experienced. It took years for me to understand that many of my choices in life had been made, not in accordance with what I would have chosen for myself, but as a reaction to mistakes I'd seen others make.

Inventory Your Beliefs

Let's look at some of the beliefs upon which you have based your drive to do it all, all by yourself:

- I believe that asking for help is

  _____

  _____

- I believe that I should be able to do it all because

_____

_____

- If I let others help me, I will

_____

_____

- I believe I can only depend on

_____

_____

If you are what you believe, then what you believe is vital to your sense of self-worth, self-acceptance, and ultimately self-trust. Evaluate what you wrote. Do you see a lot of negative beliefs? Can you see how negative beliefs can sabotage any effort you make to change your course and can keep you stuck in self-sufficiency?

If you answered yes and again are ready, willing, and able to invest in a better path, here are some steps with examples you can practice to change a belief that is self-sabotaging.

1. Become aware of the belief that is holding you back.
   - Asking for help is a weakness.
2. Rewrite the belief; post it where you will see it every day.
   - Asking for help is a strength.
3. Focus on the positive nature of the new belief, not the negatives that will keep you from doing it.
   - The positive is this: if you do believe that asking is a strength, then it will open you up to collaboration, more fulfillment, getting more done, and all the things we talked about in Chapter Six.

4. Visualize yourself embracing the new belief.
   - How will your voice sound? Confident? What about your posture? See others reacting cheerfully to you as you ask.
5. Observe two others who are acting out this new belief in their lives.
   - What benefits do you see them receiving as a result?
   - Do they show fear or confidence?
6. Break the new belief into small actions, ones you can do even though you have never done them before.
   - Think about how you'll ask.
   - Make a list of all the changes this shift in belief can make in your life.
   - Share these realizations with someone else.
7. "Act as though" that belief is in place; "act yourself into right thinking." (We'll go into detail in Chapter Eight to show you how to do this.)
8. Act until the new behavior feels as familiar as the old.
   - This will take a while because it's your longtime belief that asking is a weakness. Practice and put the new belief into action. One day you'll wake up and wonder how you could have believed any other way.
9. Seek out encouragers to support you.
   - Some of your friends have known how to interact with the Self-Sufficient but may have trouble knowing how to encourage. Never fear. They're out there.
10. Celebrate each step along the way.
    - This needs to become a habit. It records new behavior and new beginnings every time you celebrate, no matter how small they may be. Just standing in your office and saying "Yes!" acknowledges your success.

You can repeat this process on each and every belief that is not serving you well at this point of your development. Reprogramming certain beliefs may take longer if they are deeply entrenched, but persistence pays off. When we reprogram the software that our hardware system is running, then the mind doesn't know the difference between real experience and what we're telling it. So in the visualization stage, literally utilizing the relaxation technique we talked about in Chapter Five will help you get into a state that is most ready to accept new programming. Visualize yourself going through your day, literally putting the new belief into practice. See yourself being successful with others as you use the new behavior. Favorable responses. Smiles on faces. Acceptance. See yourself surrounded by encouragers who are cheering you on.

Reinforce the message through visualization every opportunity you get. Twenty minutes a day is optimum, but any at all is better than none. This reprogramming will happen over time. You'll be surprised by how quickly you will start to see results, not only in your daily experience, but in the way you view yourself: someone who believes she has power, potential, and purpose in acting on beliefs that build her up.

You'll have every reason to trust that person to look out for your best interests in new situations, whether it means acting independently or reaching out for help. Either way, you'll know that your fulcrum is fortified by a clear understanding and commitment to act according to your values, needs, and beliefs. That awareness will help create a new template that you'll be able to transpose over everything you do and are—this is someone of value stepping up to the plate. You have a strong sense of who you are and where you're going. You no longer react—you are proactive. All because you have created a strong foundational base to leap from in faith and go back to for security.

Nothing worthwhile comes easily—or quickly. Neither does rebuilding the fulcrum foundation that supports and stabilizes each thing we do. One of my great mentors, Cleve Bachman, gave me much sage advice, but probably the most important of all was the simplistic "Time is on your side." As I've gone through difficult times in my life, that line has echoed through my brain and then my heart. One day at a time. All we can do for today is keep the awareness sharply in front of us of what has to go, and reinforce it with the right behavior, experimental though it may be, until we eventually act our way into right thinking.

Mission Accomplished!

You deserve a round of applause. You've taken the time to think through some pretty soul-searching, serious stuff. Maybe more time than you have in years . . . maybe ever! Remember that the purpose of all this introspection is to solidify your base, to make sure that whatever behaviors you choose are supported by the core *you*. As you invest in firming up your foundation, you will find the thought of asking for help less threatening. You'll be in a position to start taking calculated risks. You'll begin to feel more connected as you find appropriate moments to test out leaning on others in healthy adult dependency. How will this happen? One building block at a time. How about tools? Every building project needs them. What luck! I've got some customized tools and tactics coming up that will allow you to take all these theories and concepts and apply them "hands-on" to the real situations you face. When it's all said and done, that's the only kind of application that really makes a difference anyway, wouldn't you agree?

CHAPTER EIGHT

How to ACT:
Tactical Tools

Our deepest fear is not that we are inadequate.
Our deepest fear is that we are powerful beyond measure.
NELSON MANDELA

L et's admit it. Self-Sufficients are practical people. We will accept the need to be introspective up to a *point*—but what really interests us is how all this self-discovery relates to Monday mornings . . . you know, *real* life.

In this chapter, I'll discuss what to do at the moment of truth, when we're faced with a situation in which we can fall back on acting self-sufficiently or spring forward to enlist help and support from others. How do we make the transfer from old ways to new? At this moment of tension, this point of an unfamiliar, even awkward choice, how do we make an outward decision that reflects our inner values, needs, and beliefs? Let's practice some tactics.

Tooling Up

I want to explain two powerful, practical techniques that you can begin immediately, techniques that will allow you to tap the benefits

of interdependence. Consider putting these hardworking implements into your toolbox. The first one is *observational learning*, and
I'll compare it to a precision-quality magnifying glass. The second
technique I call the *ACT Analysis*. It's more like a Swiss army knife,
one tool equipped to come at a problem in several different ways.

Tool #1: Use Observational Learning to Shorten Your Learning Curve

Eleanor Roosevelt is reported to have said, "It's a good idea to
learn from other people's mistakes; you won't live long enough to
make them all yourself."

When you think about it, not much is original when it comes
to human behavior. Our ancestors, and theirs, struggled with the
same basic drives that we do, but in the context of their own
times. Smart people have always learned from other smart people—because it's the smart thing to do!

If you're a true Self-Sufficient, the good news is that you already
know a lot about the concept of observational learning. Sleuthing
out and latching onto the ways others achieve success has been a
useful method to avoid having to directly ask for help. You'll be
glad to know your strategy is backed up by credible social science.
Albert Bandura, an expert on observational learning, came up
with some guidelines that determine the effectiveness of this technique: we must be motivated, we must see value in what we're
observing, and we must remember it to repeat it.

Now, let's apply these guidelines to those of us stuck in the Self-
Sufficiency Syndrome by using the "if, and, then" format.

If we search out individuals who appear balanced in the practice
of appropriate self-reliance and healthy adult dependency,

And we like the payoffs they enjoy from their inter-
dependence,
And we can see how our lives would benefit from the
same results,
And we are motivated to change our current behavior,
And we absorb and remember the specific actions we saw
and admired,
Then we can change our behavior by imitating theirs.

I'll never forget one of the times I did this on purpose. Living in Dallas at the time, I had wonderful friends, Gretchen and Jack, who included me in their social life. Jack, in particular, was loved by everyone. At one event, I decided to follow him around and be a "fly on the wall." What made Jack so likeable? I knew why I liked him, but I was curious about his universal appeal. What could I learn?

As we walked into the party, Jack went up to the first couple he came to and asked about their children. "How's Danielle? Did she do well in the spelling bee? How's Sammy doing with his soccer?" After about ten minutes of catching up, he moved on and asked questions of other guests. Following him around the room for an hour, I had my answer. Almost without exception, when Jack excused himself from a small group, someone would say, "Isn't he the nicest person?" Whether this behavior was by design or just Jack's natural personality didn't seem to make much difference regarding the positive results. Making his way through a sea of people, he invariably left a trail of goodwill and admiration behind him. You can be sure this exercise of observational learning made an impression on me. What I learned by watching and emulating Jack has served me well, both personally and professionally.

So, here are a few specific tactics that I have learned that you can try out to capture the benefits of observational learning.

1. Tactic: Learn by Lurking

The way you make this tactic work for you is to start pretending. That's right, I said *pretend*—like Tom Cruise or Halle Berry, when they're in character. Don't get me wrong; I'm not saying to be phony. I'm describing the initial step in taking on a radical new behavior that will eventually be authentically yours. Ask any professional actor worth his salt and he'll tell you that studying and taking on the actions of a character in minute detail is what makes for a believable performance. He'll also tell you that this process is so powerful, it can take real discipline and mental stability not to let the character infiltrate his real life. My point? If you want to become interdependent, act as if you already are. How do you do this? You break the sacred rule of Mrs. Harris's third-grade class. . . you copy others! Yes, that's right. You search out the smartest people in the class, the company, the book club, whatever, and sit next to them, watch their every move, emulate their approach—and no, it's not cheating. It's the way that wise people have gained their wisdom over the generations. Philosopher William James is credited with saying, "It's easier to act your way into a new kind of thinking than it is to think your way into a new way of acting."

2. Tactic: Learn a Second Language (*How* to Ask for Help)

We all know people who seem to say just the right thing at just the right time and in just the right way. They are often characterized as "great communicators." Like the violin in the hands of a virtuoso, language is used as a versatile instrument, minimized for subtlety, maximized for enthusiasm, and finessed to convey love, sadness, anger, or approval. Even if we don't agree with what they say, we can learn by listening to how they say it.

When it comes to asking for help, the question I am asked most often is, "What do I say? What are the words I should use?"

My answer is always the same. You have a style that is uniquely yours, and although I can help you frame a question, I don't want to literally put words in your mouth.

I'll offer the following suggestions if you'll agree that you'll adapt them to your own style of speaking. And always bear in mind that speech is just one component of communication. Gesture, tone, facial expression, and body language often have even more impact than the words you say. The confidence you've gained by acknowledging and becoming grounded in what you value, need, and believe will serve you well as you learn the language of asking. And go ahead and *act as if* you're asking for something you deserve even if you're still working on believing that yourself.

From all my years in sales, the one idea that has proved true time after time is *people support what they help create*. Therefore, always ask in a way that acknowledges that other person's skill, schedule, and significant contribution to solving your problem.

Here are some examples for various situations:

- "Can we put together a time that we could talk about what you've learned about . . . ?"
- "Would you be willing to educate me in regard to . . . ?"
- "Would it be possible for you to show me that technique you mentioned right now as we're working on . . . ?"
- "When you learned this software program, did you have a schedule for laying out each piece? Would you be willing to share that with me?"

Say these aloud to yourself and experiment with your tone of voice. You should sound like someone who is confident, eager to learn, willing to do your part, respectful, and deserving of respect even if your request is rejected. Here are a few more examples based on the importance of asking for what you need from someone:

- "Could we figure out a time when we could just sit down and talk about this?" (Need: I need more time with this person.)
- "Let's schedule a 'date' each week to get away and be able to talk like we used to. What do you think?" (Need: I need more uninterrupted time with this person.)
- "It would help me to know what your priorities are on this list of tasks." (Need: I'm overwhelmed with everything I've been given to do and need to have a clear idea of what is important to my manager.)
- "The carnival is in two weeks and it's obvious to me that I've bitten off too much. Would you have time to put a flowchart together to keep us on track?" (Need: I'm doing it all by myself again, and I want to change that.)
- "I need some quiet time from the kids. Would it work for you to take them for an outing at the mall for a couple hours this afternoon?" (Need: I'm feeling overwhelmed and stressed, and I need to schedule a few hours of self-care.)

Do you see the pattern here? We asked for help in a way that makes the other person part of the solution. We also sought to frame each question with a request for permission.

This is something I stress in my workshops—the effect of politely asking for permission when you ask for help. Prepare for this to feel uncomfortable, because you are giving up some of the control based on the other person's response, but over time the results of politely asking for permission will guarantee you a better response.

Okay, but what if your request is denied, as it is bound to be from time to time?

A fundamental concept in sales is that a rejection to a request is not a *personal* rejection. It's about the other person—perhaps she has a deadline, is overstressed, or has too much on her mind to respond favorably. There was a time when we absorbed all rejections as personal, but no more. With a fortified fulcrum and healthy sense of self-trust, we can accept a refusal with grace and even compassion. And I'll explain in a minute why, regardless of the other person's response, you always take the opportunity to close with, "What can I do to help *you*?"

Say, did you notice that was the first time we even used the H-word in all the language above? See? It *is* possible to ask for help with dignity and elegance. Observe the great communicators who cross your path and then go and practice your own style of framing requests.

3. Tactic: Use Third-Person Perspective

Have you ever been an active player in an intense situation and simultaneously felt that you were hovering above, just watching yourself and what was going on? Actually, this is a very useful tool to practice on purpose when you are trying to understand and alter your behavior. Research reveals that people trying to make a change report more progress when they step back and look at themselves from a third-person perspective. The reason this seems to help is that we are more objective when we view ourselves as a "he" or a "she" rather than an "I" or "me." Try it. For example, you could say, "I blew my diet today" or "She had an extra helping of mashed potatoes at dinner, which pushed her over her target intake for the day."

Which version provides the most information? Which sounds more like personal failure? Which makes you feel more motivated to make a correction and carry on? Since you are probably much harder on yourself than others would be, try to step back and find the encouragement that comes from observing the situation as a friendly outsider would.

It's natural to compare ourselves with others—it's the way we have been taught to measure or categorize ourselves since kindergarten. But as is typical, Self-Sufficients carry this to an extreme. If we're with others who are good at something, we feel at the very least we need to be better—preferably the best.

Usually, this reaction is not born out of a sense of pride so much as an esteem deficit—the misconception that we have to do more and be more to be equal with others. If our performance is slightly less than others, then it's, "I'm lousy at that" or "I'm the dumb one in the group."

Our judgment of ourselves is way out of accurate calibration. We are afraid that if we don't judge ourselves harshly, we won't be motivated to do enough to change our behavior, when actually the opposite is true. Sincere encouragement is one of the best motivators. You practice it with others—how about including yourself in the circle of those you treat so well?

As you work through the Action Steps in the book, one of the greatest advances you'll make is to shift your perceptions from a negative approach: "What's wrong with me?" To a positive one: "What can I do to improve what I do well?"

Rachel Naomi Remen, author, physician, and lecturer, did this for me when she said that being a perfectionist meant looking at the world to see what's wrong. I don't want to live my life like that. Do you? Let's start practicing looking for what's right. In order to do that, try to drop back and look at yourself from the third-person perspective and ask:

- Is the person you're looking at strong, determined, and tenacious?

- Has this individual survived some amazing things?
- Did she do the best she could with what she knew at the time?
- Can you write a short story talking about this person and her strengths?
- Do you think she really wants to be more vulnerable?
- What would be your recommendation as an observer about a course of action?
- Will you be supportive and drop back to applaud?

If you apply these tactics in your use of observational learning, this tool will support your progress from Self-Sufficient to Sufficient-Self. Act your way into right thinking, and go for the gold. You'll surprise yourself as the character you're emulating gradually becomes the real thing—the real you. Encourage yourself for your effort even when you feel you miss the target from time to time. Have a mental conversation as if you were talking about your best friend: "She's getting there—see the noticeable progress compared to a few months ago? She just needs to pick herself up and keep heading toward change." Before long we may even feel courageous enough to ask for helpful feedback from our real friends. Wouldn't that be a turn of events? That's the power of observing and acting in congruence with your values, needs, and beliefs.

Action Steps: Kicking in Observational Learning

Pick out a couple of people who you think are Sufficient-Selves. You may need to refer to the list of characteristics in Chapter Five.

Observe their behavior. Watch how they interact with others. Are they interested in others? What do they do when they need assistance? Are they able to depend on others? How do they balance the energy they spend on achievement versus relationships?

Take one or two specific examples of their approach and apply them to your own behavior. After a month or so, go back and review the results. Has it made your relationships better? Have you made a move toward the middle in balancing your relationships and accomplishments?

Create assignments for yourself based on what you need to learn through observation. If you like, keep a journal to track what you're learning. See how many Sufficient-Selves you can "collect" in the course of the week.

Tool #2: The ACT Analysis

Like that Swiss army knife, this tool is versatile. It's great to pull out when you have the healthy urge to allow yourself to ask for help but still feel unsure. At times, your misgivings will be valid, and at other times, they will not.

How will you know why you're feeling the way you are at the pivotal moment when you must choose between self-reliance and healthy adult dependency? The ACT Analysis gives three implements to try that will assist you in pinpointing the problem. They are in the form of three questions:

1. What am I Afraid of . . . and why?
2. What am I trying to Control . . . and why?
3. Who am I reluctant to Trust . . . and why?

These questions will help you analyze the root of your misgivings and whether giving in to them will support your values, needs, and beliefs. They address the three hurdles—fear, control, and trust—that block most folks from breaking free from self-sufficient behavior. How so?

- We become stuck in the first place because on some level we are Afraid.
- We try to Control that fear through controlling everything in our world.
- We do this because we don't really Trust that there will be people there for us if and when we need them.

When we take the first letter of each hurdle, we have ACT, and by using the analysis questions we can evaluate what's going on with us internally and what we want to do about it. Let's start with the first hurdle, fear, and apply the first question.

What Am I Afraid of . . . and Why?

Our inner and outer worlds reflect each other. When our minds are dominated by fear, anxiety, or preoccupations with ourselves, the world may appear hostile or threatening. When our minds are at peace, the world and the people in it are beheld as a source of wonderment and delight.
JOEL AND MICHELLE LEVEY, from *Living in Balance*

Fear is a valuable, primal instinct. The fear of falling reminds us to watch our step. The fear of injury instructs us to avoid direct contact with fire or angry animals. The fear of starvation kept our ancestors on the hunt and keeps us clocking in at the job. We would be pretty bumped-up, bruised, and emaciated without the gift of primal fear.

Projected fear is not always so beneficial. It's fear we learn to project onto every new experience based on similar, sometimes traumatic, past experiences. When taken to an extreme, we can become stuck in avoiding similar outcomes at almost any cost, even if there is little risk that what we're afraid of will really happen. But preventing the possibility generates patterns of behavior that become ingrained and automatic. For the Self-Sufficient, this translates into building walls that keep his vulnerabilities from showing and resorting to doing it all, all by himself.

So, when it comes to asking for help, what *are* you afraid of? Here's some survey feedback we got from folks who answered candidly, "I'm afraid of . . ."

- bothering other people.
- rejection; being told no.
- someone taking over, doing the whole thing, and then taking credit.
- looking weak, inadequate, or just plain foolish.
- owing other people and having to pay them back.
- things not being completed the way I would like them to be.
- feeling subordinate to others.
- relying on someone else who doesn't come through.
- losing my confidence.
- losing my reputation that I can do it all.
- not asking in the right way.
- being vulnerable to others.
- not performing like I was raised I should.
- others seeing the mess I've made.
- my needs not being important enough for others to meet without my asking.
- surrendering some of my power.

How many of those clicked with you? It makes it really clear why you chose to be severely self-sufficient, doesn't it? Each of these respondents is acting out of a belief system that says there's always something to fear. As long as that's our guiding perception, we're likely to continue to live a reactive, resistant, closed life that keeps us isolated.

So let's try working our way together through a couple of our common fears. How about the classic, "I fear asking for help because I could be rejected." Instead of looking at this fear as an immovable barrier, consider how you might maneuver your way over, under, or around the fear of rejection.

1. Try revising your presentation. Maybe you need to change the way you've been asking. Framing your request in a negative context such as, "You don't have time to help me, do you?" is just plain self-sabotage. And even if you don't use those words, your tone of voice can imply the same thing, which is that you really don't expect your request for help to be worthy of a positive response. Practice changing both the language and tone so that you project an air of confidence and reasonable expectation: "I could really use some help with this and I know you're good at it. Would you have fifteen minutes sometime today to walk me through it?"

2. Be prepared to suggest ways that would make your request more doable. If the first response you get is "no," act as if they didn't mean anything personal by it. They could have a lot going on. Maybe more than you know. Try providing some options like, "Would there be a better time?" or "Could you recommend someone who knows a lot about this too?" or "If I help you with your tasks, would you have time to give me a hand with this?"

3. Offer your help regardless. Whether of not they say yes, go ahead and ask, "What can I do to help you?" Two reasons. First, this communicates that you have every intention of reciprocating when they might need *your* assistance. This gesture alone may nudge them to reconsider their availability to help you, if not now, then in the future. Second, offering help to them can actually take the edge off any rejection you might feel, because you will be demonstrating to yourself that you are still in control of your actions no matter how the other person chooses to respond.

4. Play the odds. This is a numbers game, so be bold and keep practicing your asking technique every chance you get. It will feel awkward at first, like using the opposite hand. But the more you practice, the easier it will get. I promise.

5. Celebrate your triumphs. That means not only when you get a "yes," but when you watch yourself brush off a "no" and move on without retreating back behind your old self-sufficient barricade.

Let's take one more. What if your fear is that someone else won't do the job up to your standards, and you're afraid that will reflect poorly on you? Okay, this may be reasonable sometimes, but you and I both know that often it's not.

Speculate with me. What if you're facing an important event or deadline, and instead of doing everything all by yourself while everyone else stands around and watches, you decide to suggest that you all meet together and divvy up parts of the project? Well, first of all, get ready—the whole group will wonder what happened. But then, after they get over the shock and see you're serious, they'll probably be uneasy. Why? Because they are well acquainted with the high expectations you have regarding how things get done. Aren't you the one who stayed up until 2:00 A.M. to make sure the name badges were calligraphed instead of just printed?

This would be the moment in the scenario when you would be tested. Are you serious about becoming more balanced in the attention you give to relationships as well as to achievement? Then, for that payoff, you may need to bite your tongue and adjust your expectations. If this is making you shake, remember what Ambrose Redmoon said, "courage is not the absence of fear, but rather the judgement that something else is more important than fear." That means going ahead and trying even though you're afraid.

Think with me further. What if they do get the job done, and by most standards (not yours) the results are about average? A critical moment. This is when you ask yourself if only hitting "average" really matters—in the big picture, in the economy of your values, needs, and beliefs. If it doesn't, then let it go. Believe me, my friend, I know how hard that is for a Self-Sufficient. But if you are willing to step back from micromanaging everything and everybody in your world, you have a chance to have what you want the most—to belong. Tempering your expectations to allow for less than your demanding standards is the price tag for building supportive relationships. Without a willingness to adjust your expectations, you'll remain stuck in isolation. You may be respected and admired from afar, but you'll never feel "part of the gang"—like you truly belong.

Several years ago, I picked up my monthly copy of *Fast Company*, a magazine full of innovative ideas. That particular month, they interviewed pilot and parachutist Cheryl Stearns. She holds almost every record for women parachutists, including thirty world records, and has won the national skydiving championship twenty-one times. She has made more than sixteen thousand jumps, more than any woman on the planet.

I was fascinated to read about the technique that has enabled Cheryl to hit her landing target 82 percent of the time. What skill and concentration! I e-mailed her, asking if she had taken any formalized training in meditation or visualization that supported her high rate of success. She replied that no, she had actually developed her own systematic techniques. That was the beginning of an e-friendship that eventually gave me the opportunity to ask how she ever found the courage to step out into thin air several thousand feet up. Wasn't she afraid? She shared with me her formula for facing fear, and, with her permission, I want to pass on to you her amazing story and approach.

Cheryl Stearns's Steps for Facing Fear

I started skydiving because I had a recurring dream about falling. I became so curious about what the sensation of freefall would be like, I could hardly get it off my mind. It came to the point that I had to satisfy that curiosity before it became an obsession. So, I took skydiving lessons, intending to make one jump and then be done with it. I figured if other people could do it, then I could learn to—at least well enough to manage a single jump. However, my first jump didn't have any freefall in it, so I had to do it again to reach my goal. One jump led to another, and by the time I finally had the opportunity for a really long freefall, I was in love with skydiving and never stopped. Was I ever afraid? You bet. I had to find a way to face the unknown, and the approach I came up with includes the following steps.

I learn before I leap. When I'm uncomfortable about something, I tackle that fear by moving toward it instead of away from it. By that I mean that it becomes my goal to know everything there is to know about the topic. I study, research, talk to knowledgeable people, do whatever it takes to be thoroughly educated, and then, and only then, do I take (in my case) the literal leap!

Quite honestly, during those first jumps I was scared to death. But I wasn't afraid of jumping as much as I was of riding in small airplanes. I didn't have a clue about how they worked or what made them fly, and I was petrified about takeoffs. What would I do if the engines quit? Yes, I knew I could jump out once we made 1,000 feet, but what if we never made it that high? My response to these fears was to become a "scholar" in understanding small planes. I started asking the pilot to explain all about the instruments and controls of the plane and got my friends who were licensed to fly to fill me in on how things worked and what to do in emergencies. Those strategies helped to diminish my fears . . . but not quite enough.

Not one to throw in the towel, I took my education further. Three months after I started skydiving, I started flying lessons to conquer my fear. By about the third lesson, I felt much more at ease, probably because by then I felt more in control. I knew how things worked and what to do in a variety of potentially life-threatening situations. I still had a lot to learn, but by confronting rather than hiding from what frightened me, I got over the hurdle of paralyzing fear.

I know my limits. Contrary to what people assume, I am not a daredevil. I don't let myself be driven to try something just because someone else is doing it. My approach is to step back, get the big picture, approach things carefully, and proceed only when I'm convinced it's safe.

I manage my terror with room for error. I always figure in a healthy margin of error. A precalculated safety net, so to speak. No matter how prepared I am, unexpected things can happen. If I have a malfunction, I want to have those extra 500 feet to deal with the emergency. It's critical that I remember that I can always lose altitude, but I can never get it back.

I don't consider quitting an option. I can't quit. If I quit one time, then it will be easier for me to quit again the next time things get tough. If I persist and conquer the obstacle, then I maintain the confidence that I'll be able to conquer the next one as well.

I believe in the instructive value of failure. I don't always succeed. Failing is not fun, and when I do, I make sure I gain something from the experience by choosing to see it as an opportunity for intensive education. I set out to learn all I can about how, when, and why things did not work out as I'd planned. By applying this valuable information and insight to the next go-around, I am so much better equipped to overcome the obstacle. With this perspective, failure can literally facilitate success.

———   ———

That's some pretty potent advice. Now turn the spotlight on yourself and consider how you might apply her steps to overcoming the fears that always pop up to block your progress. I think you will find as I have that as we dissect and see our fear for what it is, we take away the mystery surrounding it, and in doing so, we gradually neutralize the power of persistent projected fear in our lives.

Action Steps

Select a recurrent fear that persists in blocking your progress or often controls your behavior.

How can you learn more about it? Where did it come from? Did you inherit it? Is it your fear or someone else's?

Ask yourself what you would truly jeopardize if you changed your behavior. How would such a change improve your everyday life?

In what small, specific ways can you visualize applying your courage and "act as if" even though still afraid?

What room can you build in for error? Lowering expectations of yourself or others may be one way. Give yourself permission to fail, and rethink the process for a better outcome the next time.

Cheryl says you can't quit. For the Self-Sufficient, that means not retreating from facing fear head-on. Enduring the discomfort of the learning experience, resisting the lure of retreating back to old ways. How could you demonstrate to yourself in some current situation that you will not give in to the fear but plug away at learning how to be effective in asking for help if and when you need to?

Identify a recent event that you feel was a failure on your part and consider the valuable data you can gather from the experience—if you are ready, willing, and able to scrutinize the situation fairly. Did you ignore something important? What could you have done to ensure a better outcome in reaching your goal to become more inter-dependent? Can you identify anything in the situation that would be in your best interest to let go of? Do you see how answering these probing questions can set you up for future success?

What Am I Trying to Control . . . and Why?
This part of the ACT Analysis requires careful consideration to reap the benefits. What I have learned over time is that a subtle shift in the way I perceive something can make a significant change in the way I live my life. On occasion, those oh-so-subtle, life-changing shifts have taken me decades to make. One that made a huge difference in the quality of my life was understanding the difference between being in charge and being in control.

It's Not Always Black and White It seems to be a natural instinct—we all want to feel in control of our lives, that we can determine what does and doesn't happen to us. Yet most of us have no idea regarding what it means to be balanced in our expression of this basic drive. We tend to think of being in control as an all-or-nothing proposition—you either are or you're not.

Some of us grew up with this style of thinking. For example, if we grew up with chaos, it seemed there was no in between—it was either chaos or peace. It was good or bad. As a result we did not learn subtlety. We didn't think in shades of gray. So, this balanced control will be difficult for us. We're either in control or we're not. Letting go of some of the control while maintaining our own is a difficult lesson.

Since we only had two apparent choices, out of fear we decided to control everything. When we try to control everything, we're assuming a *huge* amount of responsibility, which in turn leads to absorbing a *huge* amount of anxiety. The menu of issues I assigned myself reads like an all-you-can-eat smorgasbord: romantic problems, career issues, marital spats, management dilemmas, financial crises . . . you name it, and it was on my plate. As unappealing as that sounds to me now, for most of my life, this approach seemed the lesser of two evils, compared to the other alternative of just surrendering myself to the untrustworthiness of other people who might neglect, ignore, judge, or disappoint me. No, I could see no better alternative than controlling everything, and this approach became my default setting.

In directing anyone and anything that crossed my path, I felt I was providing a useful, worthwhile service. The reflection I saw in my distorted mirror was that my supervision was altruistic and absolutely essential for everyone's good. This naturally led to a feeling of being indispensable. "What would she possibly do without my direction? Her life would fall apart. At times, I feel like I'm the only thing that's holding things together. She doesn't have a clue." Feeling indispensable fed my self-esteem and my sense of deservedness. The price tag for this kind of control, however, was dealing with the utter exhaustion I felt most of the time.

Consult a few psychologists and you'll learn that there are all kinds of behaviors that are motivated by a desire to gain or maintain control, some so subtle they are hard to recognize. A short list of some of the more common maneuvers might include:

- The individual who is proverbially late. Sometimes this habit can be fueled by a need to assert control over when things get started. Same thing for the coworker whom you can count on to walk in late to any meeting. Even if you start without him, he controls the moment when everyone has to acknowledge his entrance and catch him up.
- The person who always insists on driving, and if for some reason she can't, she assumes the copilot/navigator role by generating a nonstop litany of advice and directions to "assist" the driver. Another version of this would be the

passenger who makes it his obsession to challenge the accu-
racy of the computer navigational system on every single
turn of an entire road trip, causing his fellow travelers to
consider hitchhiking to preserve their remaining sanity.

- The friend who seems driven to monopolize every conversation. Getting a word in edgewise requires athletic skill.
Maybe she indeed thinks that what she has to say is simply
more interesting than anyone else's contribution could be,
but along with the obvious bloated ego issue, how much of
that obnoxious behavior is just about maintaining control?

- The beloved relative who always has to change tables in a
restaurant. As everyone else is getting settled, already
unfolding their napkins, he is still craning his neck for better locations, summoning the hostess for assistance in moving the entire party to a better view or away from the
kitchen. All he wants, he swears, is to make sure his loved
ones are comfortable! He has no comprehension of how
excruciatingly annoying it can be to be on the receiving
end of such "kindness."

- The natural "crisis manager" with the reputation of being
unflappable in an emergency, steady as a rock in the face of
disaster. No doubt this is an admirable quality; however, it
is possible for this individual to so identify herself by this
trait, that she creates the very crisis that highlights her skills.
Maybe not on purpose, but with the same results: she has a
need to control that is outside the range of normal.

It's natural to feel testy with these types of individuals, but to a
greater degree what I feel is compassion. I now automatically
think, "I wonder what she is afraid will happen if she steps back
and releases the reins?" For the Self-Sufficient, taking too much

control is an overreaction to a perceived security threat. The great paradox in all this is that *by being so driven to stay in control, we actually prove that we're not.* We cannot control the extreme nature of our need to be in control, or as Thom Rutledge said in his wonderful book, *Embracing Fear*, "To be addicted to control is to be endlessly out of control."

Taking Charge Versus Taking Control of Your Life—The Big Shift

The small shift in my thinking that changed everything for me was understanding the difference between taking control and taking charge. In contrast to the extreme, out-of-control need to be in control I've been describing, I define taking charge as a balanced approach that enables us to discern what we can control and releasing what we can't. We realize we can't control everything, but we can take charge of our choices, our attitudes, our goals, our actions, our reactions, and our interactions with others. The key difference in this shift is that we accept the line of demarcation: we cannot control or change these very same things in others. To do so impinges on their birthright to take charge of their own lives.

One of the simplest, most powerful models I've ever found for this was designed by Cynthia D. Scott and Dennis T. Jaffe in *Managing Personal Change* (see Figure 8.1). With their permission, I want to share with you their Power Grid model, which I have taught and found to be so effective in workshops for many years.

MASTERY As you can see, the grid is sectioned on the top into Can Control and Cannot Control, and on the left into Take Action and No Action. The first quadrant to the extreme top left is Mastery. This is something Self-Sufficients know a lot about. It's our autopilot response to new challenges: I don't care what I have

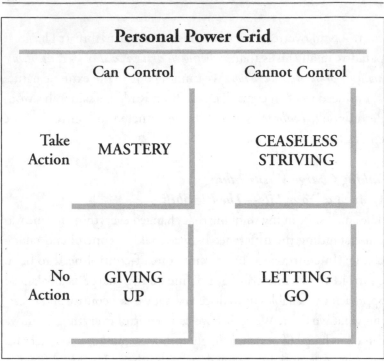

Figure 8.1: The Personal Power Grid

to do, how long it will take, how many nights' sleep I'll miss—I'll master this or bust! But here's the rub. The model says what we can control and what we can take action on. We've operated on the assumption that it's possible to control everything. To master everything. Now, it's plain to see we'll have to distinguish between what we can control and what we can't, and then we'll have several other options.

Here's your Mastery assignment: the only person you can truly control is yourself—and just focusing on *that* objective takes a lot of work. If you scored high on Self-Sufficiency Syndrome in Chapter Four, the assessment chapter, you identified strongly with the detriments we listed in continuing this lifestyle, and if you have come to accept that some modifications need to be made in your behavior, then the mastery of this will be your assignment, realizing that something has to change. And that something is you. How do you start?

- *Get educated like Cheryl Stearns suggests.* If you've read the book this far, then hopefully you can check this one off. I hope you have enough information about Self-Sufficiency Syndrome to evaluate whether this is a problem that's blocking your personal growth and to see what the payoffs could be if you made some adjustments to your thinking and behavior.
- *Applaud your courage for being willing to tackle the trial-and-error process of becoming more interdependent.* You know you can't be a master without first being an apprentice. Making mistakes comes with the territory of new learning, and failing can prep you for change like nothing else. Like a garden that's been tilled, the soil is soft and ready to receive the seeds that will result in healthy new growth. Trust me, I'm not saying it's fun to fail. But as we accept and forgive ourselves and applaud ourselves for getting up and trying again, we'll develop an inner support that over time will enable us to recover quicker from setbacks and with our self-esteem intact. Granted, it may take a while before you feel okay about revealing your mess-ups to others, but as you learn to trust your own supportive reaction when you fall short, you will feel less threatened to open up about your "constructive learning experiences" (failures) with others.
- *Become a student of your own behavior.* Using your skills in observational learning, make a conscious effort to step back and really notice what you do and why you do it—and take

notes. Quiz yourself with courageous questions like, "Why am I trying to control this person or this situation? What am I afraid of? Is my fear really justified? What's the worst that could happen if I just let go? Would I still be okay if that happened?"

- *Start with the small stuff.* Initiate some of the tactics for letting go of control and requesting help in situations where there's not a lot at stake. Look at this like after-school football practice. If you stumble or fumble, you won't be happy about it and you may go home with a bruise or two, but it's all for the sake of playing well when it really counts. As you practice and increase your mastery of asking for help in situations where the risk of negative consequences is low, you'll gain confidence and insight that will prepare you for the "big game."

- *Keep doing what works, more and better.* This is when your self-sufficient skills serve you well. You know how to focus in on a target and persist until you get it right. When those amazing moments occur when you see yourself defy precedent and resist the urge to control, try to freeze the frame mentally and later review what you did or thought that worked for you at that moment. How can you apply this to your behavior in general? Did a relationship get stronger, did a situation improve, did your values get supported by the way you acted or responded? If the answer is yes, then congratulations! Now, you replicate these moments and practice, practice, practice your way to mastery.

CEASELESS STRIVING This is such a good description of how many Self-Sufficients live their lives. The phrase conjures up the all-too-familiar feeling of trying too hard to control too many things that we actually have no real control over. Dr. Scott calls it "spinning your wheels." I call it "hitting your head against a brick wall"! We'll never succeed in this stage because we are constantly taking action in areas we cannot control. It reminds me of Mary.

Lovely, tall, and slender, Mary was a fifty-ish woman whom everyone in the workshop liked immediately. In the session when we examined the Power Grid, I asked the class to share situations that were causing them stress. Mary, who had already identified herself as a Self-Sufficient, spoke up about her mother who was very ill and lived away in Chicago at the time. She was so constantly worried about her mom that Mary was losing sleep, losing weight, and having trouble keeping focused at work. As a Self-Sufficient, she was used to taking care of everyone, and tears came to her eyes as she told the group how guilty she felt that she couldn't be in Chicago with her mother.

Thanking Mary for being so open, I suggested that the group ask her questions.

"Is your mother in a nursing home?" one participant asked.

"No, my two sisters take turns taking care of her at home."

"Do you visit?"

"Oh yes, as often as I can."

"What can you do that you're not doing?" another queried.

"I can't think of anything," Mary responded, sitting up a little defensively in her chair. "I send packages, I call, and I go as often as I can."

It was quiet, and then after a few moments, a look of new insight came over Mary's face. "I have to let go, don't I? I see that I'm doing everything possible, and trying to control the rest by worrying. I'm ceaselessly striving!" The group broke into applause.

Taking charge of your life means investing your energy in what you can control in life and limiting your participation in what you

can't. When I accepted the fact that I couldn't really change anyone but myself, I worried that if I stood back and just watched my
loved ones struggle with gut-wrenching problems, they wouldn't
think I loved them. It took me a long time to realize that just loving them and praying for them was "something." That it can be
even more loving to stand back and respect another person's learning process than it is to experience the relief felt when donning a
red cape, diving in, and saving the day. I came to appreciate that
there is a plan for others that may have nothing to do with me, no
matter how important I might want to feel. Striving to control
such situations is not only fruitless, it can actually hinder someone else's growth.

I have a dear friend whose son relied on her every time he got
into debt. Time after time, she bailed him out, and that made her
feel good until she realized that she wasn't really helping him at
all. So she stopped her rescue efforts, and he was furious. He
blamed her as things got worse. In the past, she would have
accepted the blame and out of guilt probably given in, but not this
time. He was baffled. He had been conditioned to expect a certain pattern of behavior from her, and when that pattern suddenly changed, he didn't know how to deal with it. He had the
common reaction to his mother's attempt to change—he tried
guilt and manipulation to pull her back to the status quo. With
a great deal of support from friends, she held her ground, continued to let him know how much she loved him, and expressed her
confidence that he would work out his own solutions. He did—
in his own way and in his own time. Today he is out of debt and
buying a home.

The question for my friend through this whole ordeal was that,
even though it would have been emotionally easier to repeat her
past behavior and continue fixing his problems, was that truly in

his best interest? Did it help him develop a sense of his own financial responsibility? Would he have any reason to be proud of his accomplishment? Would he have the satisfaction that comes from solving a difficult problem? Would he have confidence that he could handle problems in the future? I admired the way she came to realize that she was doing him no favors by trying to control his life, even with good intentions and a benevolent heart. I was reminded of the weight that was lifted from my shoulders when I accepted what was and was not my responsibility. "You mean I don't need to figure out their lives? I don't have to be ready with sage advice at three o'clock in the morning? I don't have to do all their work and mine too? You mean it's enough that I just take charge of my own life?" Ceaseless striving ends when you allow yourself to make good choices about what you can and cannot control and then act accordingly. Then you have taken charge by releasing control.

GIVING UP Interesting, isn't it, that we Self-Sufficients can gloss over the quadrant on Giving Up? Because we can't give up. Tenacity seems to be issued to us as standard equipment. Although an admirable trait, there can be moments when not being able to release our grip on something contributes to the problem. Because we Self-Sufficients can't allow ourselves to fail, we prefer to hang out in the Ceaseless Striving, beating our heads against that proverbial wall. We'd never think of giving up.

LETTING GO Letting Go is the opposite of Mastery. If we can control the situation and can take action, then we can master whatever we need to learn about it. However, if we can't control it and can't take action, then instead of staying in Ceaseless Striving, we need to move on to Letting Go. This remains the very toughest challenge for me.

The good news/bad news quality of our tenaciousness bears repeating. It is one of our greatest strengths, but taken to an extreme, it becomes a weakness. It will not allow us to fail. Letting go feels like failing to us. We need to come to understand that there are times when the act of letting go is the accomplishment. Giving up is when we can control but don't apply ourselves. Letting go is when we can't control, can't take action, and choose to let go rather than stay in Ceaseless Striving.

When We Let Go, We Allow the Adventure to Happen I've always loved to read since the moment I learned how. I guess it's partly because as a child, I could rely on the constancy of books. No matter where we moved, I could go to the store or library and that same series of books would be there. I preferred mysteries and for a long time was fully captivated by the Nancy Drew books. There was nothing I loved better than pitting my resourcefulness against that of the author. Her writing filled my mind and imagination with adventure. Her books became my friends.

Within each of us exists a childlike curiosity, a desire to explore new territories, discover new horizons, and be surprised about what is around the next bend. How long did it take me to see that instead of letting others create their own adventures, I was assuming authorship of their story? That I had the ending carefully crafted for them, and "for their own good" I would orchestrate the directions to that end? That I allowed no sense of adventure to exist for anyone if they listened to me? How long? Too long.

The carefully crafted scripts that I wrote for my life and everyone else's were created out of my excessive expectations of how things "should" be. It was a milestone for me when I let go of the self-imposed responsibility of creating everyone's perfect story and put my trust in something greater than myself to take care of the script writing. What I learned and continue to learn is the value of standing back and observing the incredible things that can happen when I choose to control less, fear less, and trust more. It's often just a matter of simply getting out of my own way!

Action Steps

1. Take a small baby step in taking charge while releasing control. For example, maybe you consciously choose to bite your tongue before you automatically tell someone what they really should do. If you talk fast, like I always have, you'll have to slow down consciously to be able to take a look at your thoughts before they leave your mouth. Seriously. I call this editing. Eastern philosophy calls it mindfulness.

2. Be prepared for feelings of less importance. Maybe you'll feel like you're failing the people who have always counted on you to tell them what to do. Allow yourself to stand back and watch them muddle through whatever it is and experience the joy of their own accomplishment. Or maybe you'll feel a little disappointed by how adequately everyone gets on without your advice. Instead of moping, focus on the freedom this allows you to participate in the adventure that you really have the greatest influence over—your own!

3. Get together with a like-minded person and let him know that you want to make some changes and you need another human being to help you monitor the progress. Then celebrate the fact that you were able to ask someone for help.

4. Over time, add a few more people to your group. The changes you want to make can't be done by yourself. You

cannot develop healthy adult dependency if you're not associating with some emotionally healthy adults. Interdependence can only be developed within some sort of community.

Who Am I Reluctant to Trust . . . and Why?

How can we use this third and last question of the ACT Analysis? Well, imagine that you're standing in the middle of the seesaw. There's a large project lying ahead. Your natural tendency is to turn toward your independent side, and maybe that's okay—perhaps this situation is best handled by your acting self-reliantly. But as a recovering Self-Sufficient, you want to make sure that the reason you're choosing self-reliance is not because you're reluctant to trust anyone but yourself. So you decide to use the trust component of the ACT Analysis first and make sure you're on track with some probing questions, starting with the most fundamental:

1. Do I need help but am just afraid to ask?
2. If so, why am I afraid?
3. Am I afraid to trust that other team members will do the job well?
4. Do I have a sound basis for this fear or is it projected from some unrelated experience in my life?
5. Even though I know help is available, am I resorting to the familiar feeling of security that comes with doing it all myself no matter how many hours or how much sleep it costs?

That's good for starters. Bearing in mind that as Self-Sufficients we're more prone to choose to perform solo as our default position, it's a good idea to make sure we're taking advantage of every appropriate opportunity to get practice in collaborating. What is an appropriate opportunity? Well, to tell the truth, this is another thing we must risk learning by trial and error. However, at the end of this chapter, there's a simple litmus test you can use when you are first starting out.

When you want to make a conscious effort to exercise your trust muscles in your interactions with others, the Guidelines for Trusting Others (see following page) will help you mitigate the risks.

Collaboration: To Be or Not to Be? The beauty of moving toward the balance of interdependence is that you develop the skill to decide the most advantageous way for you to pivot on a case-by-case basis. One situation in the morning may obviously lead you to ask for help from available sources, whereas another challenge could arise in the afternoon that you feel would be to your advantage (and in alignment with your values, needs, and beliefs) to handle on your own.

Regarding whether or not to collaborate, here is that litmus test you can use at the moment of decision on a case-by-case basis.

If you feel that collaborating with others will make the job

- easier,
- quicker,
- more efficient,
- less stressful, and
- produce a satisfactory outcome or
- build a valuable relationship,

then take advantage of the opportunity to enjoy depending on others rather than doing it all, all by yourself. *On the other hand*, if you sense that building a collaboration in this particular case would:

Guidelines for Trusting Others

- Use the strength of your newly trusted intuition as you make decisions about who to trust.

- Observe and assess whether an individual does what he says he'll do when he says he will do it. Is he consistent in his actions? Is he a man of his word?

- Consider how well you know an individual. Does it appear that you share some common values, needs, and beliefs? If so, that bodes well for building mutual trust. If not, there will probably be a limit to the comfort you have opening up with this person. Sure, this takes time to assess, but often you'll have a gut feeling from the get-go. Trust that instinct.

- Are your communication styles compatible? Communication is the gateway to trust. The more effectively you communicate with someone, the more information you have to make a prudent decision regarding whether and how much to trust.

- Does she have knowledge and competence in the area where she'll be trusted to act? If she has little knowledge in this area, it would be downright unfair to put your trust in her to accomplish the project with you—and unfair to her as well.

- Does he demonstrate a win-win attitude or does he act like he's out for number one? Those who think win-win are thinking about how you can benefit as well as themselves. Your growth as a person is important to them.

- Do you sense that she's willing to share knowledge? On teams today, this is a key issue. Information is power in today's market, and many see knowledge and skill level as job security. She may interpret sharing knowledge as forfeiting power or security. It's very difficult to trust someone who's not willing to share knowledge. It's a pretty good guess that they're operating out of fear or their own agenda.

These guidelines aren't foolproof. People will surprise you in positive and negative ways. But they provide a good screening tool in assessing trustworthiness that will hopefully help you feel more secure in venturing into healthy adult dependency and collaboration with others.

- create more work,
- take more time,
- be less efficient, and
- as a result be more stressful,
- this may be an appropriate occasion to rely on your own resources to get the job done.

You can choose. You are interdependent. You have options. You can shift your weight at will on that seesaw, supported by the strength of your fulcrum. The end result will be enjoying a balanced state of belonging and competency based not just on how you perform on any given day, but on who you are at your core.

Action Steps

1. Choose someone who is new in your life—maybe a new team member. Go down the checklist and evaluate this person's trustworthiness. Maybe you haven't talked with her long enough to be able to decide. Is she someone who might be a potential friend? Someone to add to your network? If so, give it a chance. Find more opportunities to talk, visit, compare notes, and get to know each other. This is a process, not an end result. Trust is built, one important layer at a time.
2. Think of someone you've known who was not trustworthy. If you had gone down the Guidelines for Trusting Others sooner, what would you have discovered?
3. Now, observe yourself. How do you rate on the checklist? How do others view you? If you were evaluating yourself through someone else's eyes, what sort of "trustworthiness"

score would you get? What action can you take to be
more trustworthy?

4. Find someone who is able to trust others and study that
   person's behavior. Ask him for his secret. Has he
   always been able to trust? Why? What helps him decide
   whom to trust?

So, my friend, you're packed with tools and tactics! Use them
and you'll go far on your journey toward the middle. That's a
promise from one fellow traveler to another!

CHAPTER NINE

Call to Action:
Networking

All persons are caught in an inescapable network of mutuality;
tied in a single garment of destiny. Whatever affects one
directly affects all indirectly. I can never be what I
ought to be until you are what you ought to be;
and you can never be what you ought to
be until I am what I ought to be.
This is the interrelated structure of reality.
REV. MARTIN LUTHER KING, JR.

This final tool is in many ways the most important. For us Self-Sufficients longing to be Sufficient-Selves, it is a key that will open many doors that have been locked by our own fears. This key is networking.

In the most practical of senses, it will allow us to learn to reach out and ask for help more quickly. It will enable us to practice our "helping skills" at the same time. Self-Sufficients are perfect for networking. We're resourceful, determined, helpful, caring, and never give up!

Networking embraces all the tenets of interdependence. All who participate recognize that working together is more productive and satisfying—that they can get information and resources faster by asking others. They realize that paying back the favor actually saves time because it's building "social capital" for the next request.

Transition from Independence to Interdependence	
Independence	**Interdependence**
"They probably don't have time."	"I call on people in a way that respects their time."
"I can do this myself."	"I work efficiently and effectively with others."
"I know what needs to be done here."	"I run my ideas by others to check my thinking."
"I don't want to bother people.	I acknowledge others by asking and including them.
"I don't know them well enough to call."	"I will expand my network by calling on people."
"They probably don't know anyone."	"I'll never know if I don't ask."

Figure 9.1: Transition from Independence to Interdependence

Donna Fisher is a professional speaker, trainer, and author. In *People Power*, she itemizes some of the shifts in thinking one has to make to transition from independence to interdependence as shown in Figure 9.1.

All the years I was a Self-Sufficient, I still saw the immense value of networking. I have wondered many times how I allowed myself to network when I couldn't ask for help. Here's what I decided. One of the primary principles of networking is that it's reciprocal. If you do something for me, then I owe you one, and vice versa. Well, I "paid back" in spades. Reciprocity took on new meaning. We've already talked about Drs. Clark and Mills and their "exchange relationship," where one gets back for giving to the other, quid pro quo.

That's an economy I could work within. If I was paying back, I wasn't really putting myself on the line, showing my weaknesses. This was an economy where information was reciprocally traded. I could network my way to new business, new clients, jobs, and resources, and never lose my professional image—never have to share who I really was. I didn't feel out of control.

I can hear the objections coming from some quarters. "I'm not outgoing. I consider myself shy." Go back to Chapter Eight and review the concept of "acting as if." Just give it a try—one baby step at a time—because if you tend to be shy, you can still leap tall buildings with the skill of networking.

Increasing Your Community

Remember Cheryl Stearns and her Steps for Facing Fear? I "met" Cheryl because I e-mailed her. My initial question could have been answered, period, end of story. But I was fascinated by what she was doing. I could never jump from a plane. What made this woman tick?

After many e-mails, I learned more about her. She is so likeable, so approachable and willing to help. After I moved to North Carolina, Cheryl and I realized we lived right down the road from each other. I'll never forget the sunny Saturday I stood at our little Hendersonville airport and watched her Cessna clear the trees. What a wonderful day we had, and I'm sure it's the first of many. How glad I am that I e-mailed.

It's all about consciously embracing the members of your community. Let them know who they are. Let them know how much you appreciate them—how much they have contributed to your life and how much you would like for them to be part of your personal community.

Does that description touch something inside? We can have that. But in the midst of our disconnected world, it's up to us to make it happen.

The Practical Side of Networking

It's been estimated that each of us knows from five hundred to one thousand people. Does this surprise you? It seems unrealistic until you really give it some thought. Neighbors, schoolmates, teachers, friends, church members, dentists, doctors, insurance and accounting professionals, fellow employees, vendors, and so on—we have a relationship with each of these even if it's just name identity. What sort of far-reaching power does this have for us?

Why Networking Works

While networking, we are utilizing these relationships to gain information. Networking is all about information even though most of us think of networking as about people. It is! But we're utilizing this expanse of relationships to exchange information.

- Resources for work, play, and home
- Advice of all sorts
- Support as we go through changes
- Career information and referrals
- Finding jobs
- Creating partnerships and alliances

- Getting new business/expanding our markets
- Starting a consortium
- Finding a mentor

As relationships develop, common values are uncovered. Trust is grown; rapport is built. We borrow that trust and rapport as we borrow someone's name. That's the reason networking is so powerful. That's why it works; it can open doors for us.

A week after my daughter Sally graduated from college, she packed up her car and headed off to Los Angeles with her best friend, Lottie.

Sally didn't have an apartment or a job, but she was rich. She had been asking anyone and everyone for months if they knew anyone who lived in L.A. or if they had a contact in the TV industry, where she dreamed of finding a job. She left Dallas with only eight names.

Four weeks later, while having breakfast with one of her referrals, she got the lead for the job that was to occupy almost every minute of her life for the next three years.

About six weeks later, I got an urgent call from Sally. She was in pain from a tooth, had been calling dentists for an hour, and couldn't get anyone to see her. Desperate, she called her mom. I asked her to give me thirty minutes and started to think through my invaluable network. Her orthodontist came to mind. We had been in Dr. Daugherty's office every month for two years, so he definitely knew Sally.

When I explained the problem, I'll never forget his reply: "This is your lucky day! My roommate in dental school practices in L.A." An hour later, Sally was sitting in his chair.

In less than three months, Sally's life had been impacted greatly by networking and its power.

Another Dimension

Not only are we capitalizing on the relationships that exist, we're also gifted through a couple of very human aspects.

- People want to help. If you don't believe it, look at national and world disasters and what has happened. The outpouring of assistance has been amazing! I think we were all born with a "helping gene."

  On December 13, 2000, Janet Forrest's sixth-grade class at Taylorsville Elementary in North Carolina sent an e-mail to 32 people, and asked them to forward it to all their contacts, expecting to receive maybe 10,000 replies. They were curious to see where in the world their e-mail would travel. Responses: more than 450,000. Backlog of unopened responses: 440,000. Their first respondent was Dell Computers in Texas. Within an hour they were contacted by their first overseas respondent: Japan. Within hours, 76 countries responded to their e-mail.

- We have no idea who people know. Our networks reach out over such diverse areas, I am never surprised when I do what I call a People Power Exercise. For instance, in Dallas, I would ask everyone to stand who could contact a Dallas Cowboy in three contacts or less (they know someone who knows someone who knows a Dallas Cowboy). In a group of 100, on average, there would be 10 to 15 people. When I asked who could contact the owner of the Cowboys in the same way, I'd get 5 or 6. Even Margaret Thatcher, the former prime minister of England, could be reached by 2 or 3 because her son lived in Dallas.

  If I'm in another part of the country, I'll ask for those to stand who have lived in Texas or know someone who lives in Texas, and it never fails—20 to 30 people will stand. Through people, the world's information and resources are actually closer than the yellow pages, and a whole lot more fun.

Start with Your Core Group

Your core group is the center of your community—your very closest, most trusted inner circle. These are the small handful with whom you share your innermost secrets, dreams, foibles, fears, goals, and problems. They are the center of your community wherever they might be. There is trust, rapport, as well as goals and values in common. With this very small population, you feel that you belong. Because of that, here are some questions to ask yourself:

- How often are you in touch with each one? In spite of the Internet, cell phones, and so forth, we need "face time" with those within our core group. We need to see the acceptance in their eyes, hear the encouragement in their voices, and feel the welcoming of their hugs.

  What adjustments could we make to better stay in touch? Have you ever had the experience where you were so tired you felt you just needed to hibernate, to hide away from the world? Then you had an opportunity to get with a core group friend and you felt rejuvenated? Energized? Why do we see fit to penalize ourselves? Is it guilt because we are actually meeting some of our own needs?

- What can we do for them? If we're to build social capital, then feeding our networks will be the first powerful step. Being conscious of the individuals in your community, what they do, what they're interested in, what their goals are is critically important for this. As you meet new people, think "who in my community would be helped by meeting this person?" As you come across information in their field, forward it to them. If they have a service or product, be on the look-out for a potential customer. Over the years, I've had so much fun with this. When you get in the habit, things pop up everyplace. One day during the Christmas season, I was in a luggage shop that had diversified and had a little of everything. So, I wasn't surprised when a customer in front of me asked if they carried chocolate. When the salesperson said, "no" I piped up immediately, "sorry for overhearing your conversation, but I think I can help. One of my community, Kali Schneiders, is a speaker and author of a fabulous book called *Truffles from Heaven*. Of course a chocolate company has offered to supply chocolate truffles with each book." My association listings just happened to be in the car and the rest is history. The lady I met in the store did all her Christmas shopping with Kali.

More Information About Networking

In 1967, Stanley Milgram, a social psychologist, did a study that became popularly known as Six Degrees of Separation. You may know it as "The Kevin Bacon Game." Research shows that the study was never definitive in its outcomes, but it sets up a powerful idea that is further heightened by our electronic world. That through people we know, we can link ourselves to others who can send us on our way—quickly—to our goal. I see that every time I do my People Power Exercise.

Here are a couple of tips to network well. Make sure you're clear about what or whom you're trying to network to. Remember people want to help, but they can't help if they don't know what you're trying to accomplish. This makes perfect sense when you think about it, because if we're clear, the name that person gives us will be "one closer" to where we're going than they are.

In workshops I explain that each of us is like our computer. We've got a data bank full of information and names. When networking, it's our job to put in the right key words to get the most specific information or names out. Sound a lot like Google? Exactly!

Believe in Small World Stories

Some incredible small-world stories happen to us. Jung called it synchronicity. Some call it coincidence and others say, "It's God's way of staying anonymous."

In workshops I ask for small-world stories. My rationale is this: if people can see what can happen, they'll be open to discussing what or whom they're looking for with each person they meet. I've heard some incredible small-world stories. My favorite, however, remains one from a Vietnam veteran pilot, who came up after a workshop one day to tell me his story about being shot down in enemy territory. While being rescued by a helicopter at the last crucial minute, drifting in and out of consciousness as he was lifted aboard, the numbers 7048 on the fuselage burned into his brain. He spent two years in a military hospital, then went home to recuperate from his leg injuries, where he recounted his story at a cousin's birthday party. He expressed his regret that he had never been able to thank that pilot, when a man on the other side of the table made his way around to say, "I was the pilot of 7048."

There are others out there who will accept us, help us, and then come ask us for assistance. Being asked for help in this context makes us feel we are valuable, that we have something to contribute, and that we are not self-sufficient.

Now, for the toughest part of building your personal community. At some point in the conversation, you'll be asked, "What can I do to help you?" Here is the moment of truth. Can you rationalize reciprocity in your mind to see the even exchange and be able to take part?

Networking Enhances Our Soul

Did you read the book or see the movie *Pay It Forward*? This is the concept we're after. That, at some point, networking will transcend the reciprocal and take on a spiritual meaning. All of a sudden you'll be helping and asking for help interdependently as a result of personal growth, not reciprocity. There's even a name for these relationships.

Drs. Clark and Mills called this spiritual relationship a *communal relationship*. The idea to help and be helped will become so ingrained that it will become second nature, and the desire to pass it along and do something for someone else will grow as you grow toward your highest potential. I'll support your goals and in so doing, I'm supporting a vision of building community—something larger than ourselves.

That will be the beginning of the end of your Self-Sufficiency Syndrome. You'll never want to go back again.

Action Steps

1. Be aware that, one more time, you'll be stepping out of your comfort zone if you've never networked before. You might want to go back and review Chapter Five to prepare yourself.

2. Who's in your core group? Make a list and let them know they are part of your new community.
3. Find a successful networker and utilize your observational learning.
4. Ask for help within your core group.
5. Be accountable to those in your core group for your progress.
6. Constantly expand your network to include those who can help others.
7. Feed your network; look for ways to help those in your community.
8. Be aware when your "exchange relationship" turns to a "communal relationship." That's interdependence!

The world is changing at warp speed. We have two choices: change with it or choose some other course of action. I vote for the "other course of action"—to strive for balance in an unbalanced world. In order to do that, we'll have to face being different, going against the tide, but it may be the only way.

In Kathleen A. Brehony's incredible book, Living a Connected Life, her call to action is articulate and appropriate to this particular conversation.

We've seen just how critical our need is for connection and belonging. If we are to truly awaken, we'll remember just how much our human species needs one another. Remember infants die without warm and loving relationships, and so will we. Each of us must find our own connections, but collectively we must reevaluate the cultural and civic institutions that create containers for all of us in which we will thrive or perish. And we'll have to walk the walk and not just talk the talk. Those values we prize will have to become everyday actions.

And the situation is urgent. We can no longer afford the disconnects between what we say we believe about living a meaningful life and how we behave. We can no longer afford the luxury of saying that we are compassionate without demonstrating kindness, saying that we are a united people without embracing each other, or believing ourselves to be patriotic without being willing to sacrifice for our freedoms, beliefs and one another. We'll have to live with this new consciousness at the top of our minds and expressed in the particulars of everyday life as we forge a new way of living together.

We have an unparalleled and soul-searching opportunity to rethink our values and priorities and draw from our vast knowledge about how human beings can learn to live together with a respect for the full dignity of the individual while at the same time revering our human needs for one another and for safe harbors for everyone. Together we can awaken the ancient stirrings of our souls and recreate our lives and our communities in ways that allow love to flourish. Each of us can encourage our human potential and all of our chances for living a full, rich life by remembering that we all share a single web of existence and that separateness is a dangerous illusion. We'll take a hard and honest look at our own lives and relationships. We'll assess where we are strong and where we need to work harder to build the kind of fertile safe harbor of friends, family, and community that will provide a container for our own psychological and spiritual growth.

You can do this. All the internal and external tools I've shared work. They've worked for me—and many others across the country. It takes awareness and acceptance of where you are today and where you want to go. It takes willingness and preparation to begin. This may become your greatest undertaking!

Conclusion

We need a renaissance of wonder.
We need to renew, in our hearts and in our souls,
the deathless dream, the eternal poetry, the
perennial sense that life is miracle and magic.
E. MERRILL ROOT

This may be the end of this book, but it's only the beginning for you. Awareness is a wonderful light. It obliterates the shadows and allows you to see clearly into the crevices of your life where you are being held captive. It releases you from being walled off from the opportunities that await you. I hope in some small measure this book has served to shed light on that awareness for you.

We tend to forget that we're not here alone, that we were never intended to be here alone. It is our own thoughts, beliefs, behaviors, and fears that act as a block to our birthright. Let's turn those stumbling blocks into stepping-stones.

We've looked at the developmental stages that were to have prepared us brilliantly for our connection to the world. And hopefully, you've been able to see where people just like you, deprived of that basic training, couldn't give it to you. Perhaps you've been very angry and resentful about that, rationalizing it as the reason you haven't been able to do this or that. If you choose, it will always be there as that excuse for not living your life full-out.

But if you make another choice, you can choose to activate your courage and go back to pick up the missing pieces you left behind. As an adult, you will find so many skills, talents, and tools that you never had before. It will become a proactive process with you in charge to choose to develop a new level of trust and reciprocity and desire for collaboration that were to have been a part of that very first stage. It's a makeup test that may end up having more meaning and quality than it ever would have had in the beginning, because it will be hard-won. You know how we Self-Sufficients are about accomplishment.

These missing pieces of the puzzle have kept us from being able to see that whole picture, that this life is much about what we learn and how we grow, who we become through our connections with others.

We took a long look at what Self-Sufficiency Syndrome is. My hope is that you were able to see how the behavior has been good to you; in some cases, it actually allowed you to survive. But like old clothes, worn much too long and threadbare, it's time to let go of the old and bring on the new. Remember the life-preserver image from Chapter Two? It's time to take it off and learn how to live in collaboration on dry land.

And it's not about doing it perfectly according to unrealistic expectations of ourselves. There will be times when under stress we'll default to the old behavior that has been with us so long, and we'll need our own understanding, compassion, and empathy to allow us to pick right back up and do it all over again—this time with the help of others.

We stopped in to visit our "ready, able, and willingness" and how important that is to the success we have chosen. Without this stage of "preparedness," it's so easy to fall back into old ways, but having thought all of it through, we can learn to live in the world of "we," not "I."

Then we looked at the actual mechanics of change and transition and what that means to us as we move forward. Realizing that our comfort zone hasn't been all that comfortable should motivate us to build a new one. Change can be positive and good even when we're not controlling it.

Fear, control, and trust—the triumvirate of our dilemma! If we can learn to balance these in a healthy way, we'll be able to take our feet off the ground and participate in a world that's not always consistent, predictable, and controllable. By taking our feet off the ground, we'll be capable of experiencing the adventure of our lives, free of unrealistic fears. Trust will have become the bridge that allows us to connect with others. The ACT Analysis will serve you well. When you find yourself trying to do it all, all by yourself, these questions will help you sort it out. Is it because I'm afraid of something or someone? Is that why I'm trying to control this situation? Is trust an issue? Is there good reason not to trust this person who wants to help? Or again, is it about my fear? Which brings you full circle—ACT.

The greatest tool, of course, is others. When we still doubt ourselves, our choices, and their wisdom, another perspective from around the campfire is the best medicine in the world. As we seek advice and counsel from others we trust, we are experiencing the byproducts of support and encouragement that remind us we are not alone.

When we make the shift in thinking, we awake to realize that, if we turn inward, that very act of courage will prevent us from returning to the way we were. Robert Frost's words echo in my heart—"the best way out is always through." We will have made a monumental decision to look at what's holding us back. Often this will also necessitate looking at old baggage that's been holding us down on that seesaw like so much ballast on a ship.

Will it be hard work? Like you could not have dreamed. But isn't that our greatest talent? Won't we be pulling out the determination, persistence, focus, and drive to achieve that have made us so successful as Self-Sufficients? You bet!

Interdependence—community. Not only the third stage of our individual development as a human being but also the culmination of the important lesson we are meant to learn. We come into this world alone; we leave alone. What we learn, how we will contribute, and what we will become is measured by our relationships while here. That's the promise and that's the adventure!

Bibliography

Chapter One

Bowlby, John. *Attachment and Loss: Separation: Anxiety and Anger.* New York: Basic Books, 1973.

Brazelton, T. Berry, M.D., and Stanley I. Greenspan, M.D. *The Irreducible Needs of Children: What Every Child Must Have to Grow, Learn, and Flourish.* New York: Perseus Books Group, 2000.

Karen, Robert, Ph.D. *Becoming Attached: First Relationships and How They Shape Our Capacity to Love.* New York: Oxford University Press, 1994.

Lerner, Richard M. *Concepts and Theories of Human Development.* 3rd ed. Mahwah, NJ: Lawrence Erlbaum Associates, 2002.

Main, Mary. "Introduction to the Special Section on Attachment and Psychopathology: 2. Overview of the Field of Attachment." *Journal of Consulting and Clinical Psychology* 64, no. 2 (April 1996): 237–43.

Noam, Gil G., and Kurt W. Fischer, eds. *Development and Vulnerability in Close Relationships.* Mahwah, NJ: Lawrence Erlbaum Associates, 1996.

Santrock, John W. *Topical Life-Span Development.* 2nd ed. New York: McGraw-Hill, 2005.

Chapter Two

Peck, M. Scott, M.D. *A World Waiting to Be Born: Civility Rediscovered.* New York: Bantam Books, 1993.

Chapter Three

Basco, Monica Ramirez, Ph.D. *Never Good Enough: Freeing Yourself from the Chains of Perfectionism.* New York: The Free Press, 1999.

Chapter Five

Bridges, William. *Transitions: Making Sense of Life's Changes.* New York: Perseus Books Group, 1980.

Chapter Six

Bornstein, Robert F., Ph.D., and Mary A. Languirand, Ph.D. *Healthy Dependency: Leaning on Others Without Losing Yourself.* New York: Newmarket Press, 2003.

Cramer, Kathryn D., Ph.D. *When Faster Harder Smarter Is Not Enough: Six Steps for Achieving What You Want in a Rapid-Fire World.* New York: McGraw-Hill, 2001.

Chapter Eight

Bandura, Albert. *Self-Efficacy: The Exercise of Control.* New York: W.H. Freeman, 1977.

Bandura, A. *Social Foundations of Thought and Action: A Social Cognitive Theory.* Englewood Cliffs, NJ: Prentice-Hall, 1986.

Canfield, Jack, and Mark Victor Hansen. *The Aladdin Factor.* New York: Berkley Books, 1995.

Govier, Trudy. *Dilemmas of Trust.* Montreal: McGill-Queen's University Press, 1998.

Libby, Lisa K, Richard P. Eibach, and Thomas Gilovich. "Here's Looking at Me: The Effect of Memory Perspective on Assessments of Personal Change." *Journal of Personality and Social Psychology* 88, no.1 (January 2005): 50–62.

Remen, Rachel Naomi, M.D. *My Grandfather's Blessings: Stories of Strength, Refuge, and Belonging.* New York: Riverhead Books, 2000.

Rutledge, Thom. Embracing Fear and Finding the Courage to Live Your *Life.* New York: HarperCollins, 2002.

Scott, Cynthia D., Ph.D., M.P.H., and Dennis T. Jaffe, Ph.D. *Managing Personal Change*. New York: Crisp Publications, 1989.

Stearns, Cheryl. "Fear Model." Interview by Peggy Collins, 2005.

Chapter Nine

Brehony, Kathleen A. *Living a Connected Life: Creating and Maintaining Relationships that Last a Lifetime*. New York: Henry Holt and Company, 2003.

Fisher, Donna. *People Power: How to Create a Lifetime Network for Business, Career, and Personal Advancement*. Austin, TX: Bard Press, 1995.

Levey, Joel, and Michelle Levey. *Living in Balance: A Dynamic Approach for Creating Harmony & Wholeness in a Chaotic World*. Newburyport, MA: Conari Press, 1998.

Palmer, Parker J. *Let Your Life Speak: Listening for the Voice of Vocation*. New York: Jossey-Bass, 1999.

Quick, James Campbell, Debra L. Nelson, and Jonathan D. Quick. *Stress and Challenge at the Top: The Paradox of the Successful Executive*. New York: John Wiley and Sons, 1990.

Index